Motherlode—
Essays on Parenthood

ISBN-13: 978-1501033292
ISBN-10: 1501033298

PUBLISHER'S NOTE

For more information on upcoming anthologies, visit the website at kystory.net.

Contents

Growing Up or Not—Treg Isaacson

Growing Up

I'm standing in Lukas's dorm room with him and there's really nothing to say. Leaning on his desk next to his sleeping bag, pillow, and backpack, I look up when his roommate comes in. It appears he's come in before and they say hi or introduce themselves, as often happens in a situation like this, with young people. Like, Yeah, we're going to be spending the weekend here together, but we may not speak to each other the whole time. Or maybe we'll go through a couple trainings out on the soccer pitch and size each other up from afar, and then we'll introduce ourselves.

So I say to his roommate, "Hi, I'm Treg." He says he's "Jeff." I ask him where he's from and what his team is like and where he's been and what other schools he's looked at, and Lukas joins in. After a short conversation, Jeff walks out of the room.

We talk about Jeff and his winning team, since they beat Lukas's team and they've been to major tournaments in the country. It's not tense when we don't talk. It just seems like there's nothing more to say. I already spoke to him about how to approach the weekend and his game plan with the coach. I'm not going to say how much I love him and what he means to me, and how close I feel to him. Nor about how sad I am my boy is grown up and how much I loved spending time with him when he was little, taking him to the zoo, the Children's Museum, and the Science Center. How I still love to watch him play soccer. And where did all that time go? How did he became a man and go to college? I paid attention. I heard too many people say, "Enjoy them when they are little. You only have this time once." I tried.

Avoiding

I look into my refrigerator and nothing looks good to eat. Lukas and I decide to go to Chipotle for burritos. Actually, I invite him to lunch with me so we will be face-to-face for at least fifteen minutes. During that time, together with the time we are side-to-side in the car ride over, I'm hoping to talk to him about what he's avoiding, which, as I see it, is what's keeping him from reaching his goal, which is in turn keeping him from attaining happiness in the future. He is my son and I have determined this to be my business. Many times, he has told me he has it under control, another way of saying, "Back off, Pa. I got it."

I am his father, and I do not listen, because his happiness is important to me. Not his immediate happiness, but his long-term happiness. He needs to call the college coach and sell himself. Get his attention, not back off. Assert himself. There is no other way to get what he wants. This is his next hurdle, after all the athletic triumphs he's enjoyed and the many disappointments of defeat he's endured.

Assertiveness is his next challenge. I tell him that. I am proud of the words I have chosen.

Somehow the conversation shifts. I'll tell you how: Chipotle is next to Verizon, where we got our cell phones, and mine isn't functioning properly. He asks me about getting a new phone for myself. Mine turns itself off as a matter of course. It's in my pocket and it's done being turned on. Not a setting I have chosen for it. The battery is full. I don't poke any buttons. The phone decides. This is not a quality I despise about my phone. I never wanted a cell phone to begin with. I don't like being accessible. I'm also afraid of the electromagnetic disruption it causes next to my head when I speak and the effect on my thigh when I have it in my pocket. That second part will sound crazy to him, so I stop talking after the first part, the part about not wanting to be that accessible, which still sounds crazy to him, because he loves frequent contact with all his friends. It's more insane because I need to be available to him. I am his father.

He asks me, "What are you avoiding?"

The Moth

When I had friends who were hurting, having lost someone they cared about, I liked to make them a rhubarb pie. On that particular day, I had assembled two pies with defective crusts that let the sticky filling spill onto the floor of the oven, form a smoky lake, and catch fire. I scooped the goo with a flat spatula, burning my thumb on the rack. Smoke filled the house, setting off the alarm and my pit bull's anxiety. I slammed the oven door and grabbed my mojito to cool me while I thought. The heat in the kitchen made me thirsty. Surely the rum had been the problem from the beginning.

My dog grunted and leaned into my knee. I put a mitt on to protect my burnt thumb, took a breath, and went back to smearing syrup with the spatula. The bottom of the oven looked like an Illinois prairie burn. A big black ash floating in the air got sucked into the oven when I opened the door.

Baking those pies, I forgot the morning at Green Lake, the Dragon-slayer walk to raise money to fight sarcoma. We had pushed Lukas' friend Josh around the lake in a wheel chair. Fighting fires, I didn't have to think about Josh playing his last games of baseball at O'Dea High School, foregoing chemotherapy in order to have a last season of ball. I didn't have to remember how we all had always thought, "If any one of our boys plays in the major league, it will be Josh." I didn't have to think what a great coach and mentor his dad Kiyo was for my son. I didn't have to think how Kiyo was living my worst fear. Why did he have to lose his son?

   I couldn't avoid those thoughts once the pies were done and the fire burned out. The rum didn't work, either. I found myself in the back yard trimming the long grass with my mower. I was banging the machine into seventeen-foot tall bamboo, the stalks shaking and bamboo leaves swaying back and forth over my head. Me and my measly little eighteen-inch cordless electric mower with the rechargeable battery. I needed a gas-powered mower that could do anything, cut down that damn bamboo that kept creeping into my yard and sending up shoots. I wanted to get rid of the bamboo. Kill it all. My face was in a grimace with the sadness tearing up through my heart and throat until it flowed down my cheeks and off my chin, my body heaving with sobs. I let go of the handle and stopped pushing. The blade wound down, as did the hum of the motor.

The fire in the oven. That wasn't a black ash floating down into the oven. It was a moth that descended and flew into the flames.

The Day

Clare, Lukas, and I had driven from Seattle, arriving in San Francisco as the afternoon marine layer was carving its way through the bay and up into the hills. We watched the thermometer in the car go from 108 degrees in the valley to 58 degrees in the Bay Area.

We were tired the next morning from the drive, but more sad. Feeling heavy in our hearts. Nineteen years the three of us had been together, counting the time Lukas had been in Clare's belly, and we had formed a solid little unit, a fine family. We were driving to Rawsly's apartment in time to get to soccer practice by noon. Rawsly was the goalkeeper. Lukas and Rawsly had been texting each other, and Lukas planned to sleep on Rawsly's couch or floor until he could move into a dorm at the college. All three of us were anxious. Clare was reading directions off the Garmin, and every street was named Moraga something. I had to find a gas station.

When I got back from paying, Lukas was standing by the pump. The numbers on it were still. I smiled so big and hard at him that he laughed at me. All the love I felt for him was coming out my cheeks. I hugged him. It was going to be five minutes before we were at Rawsly's and I'd be saying goodbye to him for real, for many months. We'd unload his duffle, the plastic tub of clothes and his sleeping bag, then be on our way back to Seattle.

We reached Rawsly's, and the three of us went upstairs. He'd be sleeping on one end of a huge L-shaped white leather sofa, with another freshman soccer player on the other half. We met Rawsly and Justin, and didn't know what to say. We glanced at the 2012 Summer Olympics playing on the television. Rawsly told Lukas to suit up for practice, so the three of us went to the car to get the rest of his things. We put them down on the sidewalk. My heart got big and heavy as I wrapped my arms around him, and my eyes welled up. He felt made of metal, he was so muscular. This was the baby boy who had tucked himself up on my chest, our hearts beating together every night from the day he was born until he was six months old. He'd get hungry and go over to Clare for milk, then fall asleep between us. That couldn't have been eighteen years ago. What happened to that time? I had told myself, "This is important, so pay attention."

He was a baby boy, sleeping on my chest, with all the time in the world for us to be together, then all of a sudden, I was standing on the sidewalk in front of Rawsly's apartment, with his suitcase down at our feet, hugging him goodbye.

Sneaking

Clare and I couldn't leave after we'd dropped him off, so we drove around campus and parked, hiking a small trail overlooking the practice fields. We pushed through trees, worrying about poison oak, often sliding backwards one step for every two we took up the leaf-strewn hill in our flip-flops, so that we could peek over a fence during his first day with the other boys. I told her we couldn't stay too long, that we couldn't let anyone see us; the other players would tease him if we were seen. I made her leave before she was ready. She made me drive through a parking lot so that we could look at the field, to see him out there with the team before we started back.

Kiyo

Clare and I took two days to drive back to Seattle, and after leaving Lukas, all I could think about was Kiyo. He had to say goodbye to his son a week before I did, but Josh wasn't coming home for Thanksgiving or Christmas. He wouldn't be texting to let them know how he was doing. Josh was on their mantle in an urn with his O'Dea baseball cap on top. I drove to their house, where the front door was wide open, at 5 in the afternoon.

Both Kiyo and Deedee were inside asleep. When I yelled "Hello!" at the door, she jumped off the couch and gasped. I felt horrible. I hugged her tight and told her I was sorry. I couldn't shut up about how sorry I was for waking her, when the truth was I felt heartbroken her son was dead.

She yelled to wake Kiyo, who was lying on Josh's bed. Fifty baseball caps surrounded him just below the ceiling of the room, spanning the four walls. Under one was the plastic mask the doctors had poured molten over Josh's face to keep his head still while they irradiated the sarcoma in his jaw. The mask reminded me of Edvard Munch's painting *Scream*, pained and frightening. I made myself look at it. Josh had to wear it scared, for God's sakes. The radiation had burned his skin under the mask and made sores inside his mouth.

That goddamned tumor had grown and eaten away at his jaw and the inside of his cheek. It spidered out across his face and temple, then down into his lungs and bones.

He got a tattoo across his chest that said, "Fuck Cancer."

Josh had said, "Fuck Chemo. Fuck side effects. I'm playing baseball this spring."

He played shortstop for O'Dea High School the spring of 2012. One of the last games I saw him play, he hit a line drive into right field and got himself into a pickle, running back and forth between the bases long enough to make sure his teammate scored from second. They won.

A few weeks later, I sat in his hospital room rubbing his withered leg, studying his dry lips, watching his Adam's apple move every few seconds when he took a sedated breath. I told him I loved him and wondered what was going on inside him. A week earlier, Josh had asked Kiyo to end his pain. They had taken him to Children's Hospital to be put under sedation. Josh died about an hour after I left him to watch my son play soccer. When Lukas saw me come into the stadium, he walked across the field to let me know that Josh had passed on.

So, a couple of weeks later, when I woke Deedee and Kiyo at 5 in the afternoon, Kiyo got up out of Josh's bed to sit in the driveway with me and smoke. He asked me how Lukas was doing. I told him we had delivered our boy down to Moraga, but he wasn't settled into a dorm yet. I asked Kiyo how he was doing, considering. He told me how some people got it and others didn't, and he didn't really want to explain it. Speaking his mind was a way to grieve. Another way was to embody Josh, wearing his clothes, and getting tattoos like Josh had done.

Josh was supposed to grow into a man, stand on Kiyo's shoulders, and become even better. That's what I want for Lukas. Take some of what I have, add his own formula, and become better than I am, and make me proud.

Josh was all about baseball, and everyone knew he had enough guts, skill, and determination to make it to the big leagues. All he ever really wanted to do was play baseball. He had been a vacuum cleaner in the middle infield from the time he was a kid. One day when he was nine years old, playing second base in a tournament in Wenatchee, he had a ball hit to him so hard it knocked the glove right off his hand. He didn't give up on the play, but dropped to his knees and attacked that mitt, digging both hands in the pocket to get the ball so he could throw the runner out at first. He was frantic, but got the ball and made the throw from his knees, a step too late.

The End of the World—
Tamara Kaye Sellman

I watch my first-born glide through the processional, the flat of her blue mortarboard emblazoned with a water polo ball outlined in bright yellow glitter. She and I share a birthday and crazy mad scientist hair. Her curls fluff from beneath the silky cap despite a thousand bobby pins and a can of hairspray. I constantly repeat the lesson to her, that some things cannot be controlled.

She still tries. So do I. There's no help for being irrevocably human.

My youngest daughter is not in this audience; she's in the pit, playing cymbals for the band clustered behind the field of graduates and their proctors. She will be a junior next year. Once my oldest falls out of lens shot, swallowed in the sea of royal blue acetate marking the class of 2014, I catch her sister in my peripheral vision, steal snapshots of her counting beats with mallets. She brings tears to my eyes. She's a drummer just like her father sitting next to me, just like her grandfather, long gone now.

In 2016, our second born will be long gone, too.

My first born's best friend, Olivia, takes the stage now. Glee club darling, she plays guitar while singing sweet notes, the same winky-eyed songbird who poked at the keys of our upright player piano years ago. More tears. I think about her mom, already bawling her eyes out this morning at the Rite-Aid while looking for aspirin while I'd been there looking for glitter.

I thought I might cry, or maybe I should cry. Maybe there is something wrong with a parent who does not cry on the morning of their first born's graduation.

Instead, I went home and helped my youngest

decorate her sister's mortarboard while she napped.

My own tears don't stop now as the valedictorian steps up, a tiny girl from my first born's kindergarten class, grown into an eighteen-year-old genius, delivering a clever speech coded in Twitterese.

I laugh. I get it. I am the hip mama in the crowd. Other parents take my cue and laugh, though they don't get it. That's the way it has always been. They accept I know things they don't understand. This is not an expression of personal arrogance on my part. There are things I know that I wished I didn't know. Sometimes I play a game in the morning: I guess how deep the circles around my eyes have sunk since I last slept.

I laugh again, this time to hide my choked-up pride for someone else's daughter. The sound of it fails me—an empty, wounded breath that only I can hear, my throat knotted with nostalgia.

Finally, the best part: I see the water polo ball

image float above the rest of the caps—my first born in the first row, heading for the podium. She can't wait to get this over with. Neither can I.

No tears now.

~ § ~

A year ago, she'd considered suicide. She thought everybody hated her. She couldn't explain why.

I look at my beautiful girl. I can't explain why, either. Freckles and naturally straight teeth. Heart bursting with a compassion rendered fragile by the cruelty of mean girls, thoughtless boys, and burned-out teachers. She's a natural teacher. She loves the quirky honesty of small children and the pure hearts of the mentally disabled. Hers is a laugh that dares you think she isn't happy.

Her father and I expected a line of boys at the door the last four years. Instead, we watched movies on the couch Friday and Saturday nights with her small group of friends, all of them misfits by the predictable conformity of high school cliques. We love these kids like they are our own.

Graduation day comes as a miracle, then. Genetics from my side of the family have shaped her fate and fluoxetine and therapy intervened. Doubt continues to creep in, but she has tools today she didn't have a year ago.

And now this: she is training for a Junior Olympics water polo team, with a summer tournament slated at Stanford in August. This, despite our small-town world telling her 'No' to dreams of NCAA membership. Someone from the deep end of the pool finally echoed my lone 'Yes,' recruiting her for a coveted spot on a D-1 women's water polo team in New York. A companion half-ride scholarship came against the odds. Ironic that she wrote her college essay about clinical depression at age seventeen. She was accepted at all five schools she applied to.

Lemons into lemonade. Another lesson drilled into my children.

Sometimes, depression is a water polo goalie afraid of jumping and missing. It took a perfect stranger to throw my daughter the ball she meant to catch. And I'd been there, with a grace that surprised me, to keep her afloat.

It wasn't easy; in fact, it was hard as hell. I've paddled these waves before, but my child struggled to keep her head above water, and I can barely swim.

I was her age when I considered taking a blade to my wrist. Two a.m., late May before graduation. The paring knife came from a service station back in the 1970s when competition for space in gas lines meant free giveaways like mugs and cutlery.

It had been a horrendous day. I'd lost my track spikes to the school mower the day before, just one week before districts, where I was expected to earn a spot at the state meet. Because of this recklessness on my part—which I know now is about as normal a behavior for any teenager as anything else—my dad spent that whole day pacing the house, literally foaming at the mouth, eyes bugged and bloodshot, bitching that now he had to pay for *a new pair of Adidas that will only be used for a couple of weeks!* and *Where are we going to find track spikes at this late date in the season?* and *How could you have been so irresponsible?* and *Do you really think you will ever amount to anything by being this stupid?* Long strings of phrases like this, with creative variations, for hours on end, with him occasionally picking up and dropping a magazine or a set of keys or whatever was nearby to punctuate his disappointment. A plate was smashed.

Earlier that spring, I'd made an appeal to my counselor regarding my dad's rants and that I feared him: the counselor told me I needed to sit down and talk it out with my parents.

My own father is no different now than he was then: bipolar, untreated, extreme, and violent. I can shut him down thirty years later, if I have to. I have the tools.

All I had at that time was a gas station knife.

That night, I stopped pressing the blade flat against the blue-green delta of my left wrist when it occurred to me this effort would make life harder for my mom, who had already spent most of her life building cushions between her children and my manic-depressive father. Killing myself—or, even worse, failing at the attempt—would only add to her list of burdens.

Besides, I was angry, too… angry I evaluated my life based on my father's madman opinions. I was never that meek, self-loathing victim of parental abuse portrayed in the ABC afterschool specials in the 1980s. I suspect that, at an early age, a guardian angel had whispered the truth in my ear: that my father's violent antics weren't normal, weren't my fault, and weren't justifiable. Ever.

As I opened the cutlery drawer, I remembered two things a perceptive teacher told me back in junior high:

"Today is the first day of the rest of your life." And, "Living well is the best revenge."

Check and check.

I put the paring knife away, clenched my teeth, and decided to leave home as soon as I could.

Some things can't be controlled.

~ § ~

My youngest plays snare now. She is a soldier in black mini skirt, crisp white blouse, tight shiny ponytail and Zooey Deschanel bangs. Born on her due date. Her timing perfect. For her, every day is a beginning. Nothing ever ends, it merely leads to something more, a current into a river feeding an ocean.

For her sister, endings are risky shortcuts to beginnings. Long, tall waterfalls with huge churning whitewater storming at the bottom. Only one way down.

After the ceremony, my daughter the graduate rushes to me, insists on using my camera, but cannot figure it out, having shot pictures off her iPhone for so long.

I smile. There's a lot she can't do. She can stave off blazing shots on goal during a polo tournament, yet she has not yet learned to drive. She solves complex math equations but cannot move past literal thinking. She works as a lifeguard, but needs instructions for making mac and cheese. I deposit her paychecks for her because she has doesn't have a bank account. Her signature looks like a five-year-old's.

Like mine, her curls froth in the humidity, tendrils recoiling to the roots.

"Please? Just show me how to do it." She bats her eyes at me, smiles, holds the camera out before her with fingertips like it is a baby with a wet diaper, her words passing through clenched teeth.

Let this one thing be easy, for once.

I know this is what she is thinking, because it's what I'm thinking. Neither of us can say it aloud, though. Some wishes can never be spoken, only shared in the silence of understanding.

~ § ~

The night she'd told me she wanted to kill herself happened just twelve hours after I received news over the phone from my doctor: the MRIs taken just the day before showed pretty conclusive evidence I had multiple sclerosis. Yet another horrendous day in my life, followed by my discovery of long, obsessive texts shared between my daughter and her best friend... words that spun out in long strings, repeating the same negative feelings, except they became intense, more dramatic, until one could only read them as threat of violence and endings.

The girls had a falling out the weekend before, but instead of letting the drama deflate, my daughter compulsively fed it with anger and an ultimatum that I recognized only too well. It hit me then, the scary familiarity of her recent string of eating habits—she normally ate like a linebacker, given the calories she burned playing polo three to four hours a day—and her frustrations about teammates, schoolmates, and the proclamation all her friends hated her. As a water polo mom, I spent a lot of time with these girls, and I didn't see what my daughter saw.

Instead, I saw an old man pacing in the dark, talking incessantly in curse words and pointed accusations about something and nothing all at once. I saw the same old man, curled up in boxer shorts on his bed at three in the afternoon, crying like a baby. The downward vortex of bipolar disorder is remarkably consistent in its power to shut down a human being.

She was scheduled to meet with the vice principal the next morning with her father, as complaints about bullying her best friend—via those disconcerting texts—had been leveled against her, not by her best friend, but by their water polo coach.

I sat that night at her bedside and asked her dreaded black-hole questions about self-harm. I realized she needed more than a visit with the vice principal.

"She's just like my Dad," I told my husband, her father. I showed him the texts that landed this inquiry into bullying.

"If you think that's what she needs," he said. He didn't fight me when I called the school to let them know our girl wouldn't be in sixth period that afternoon due to a doctor's appointment.

~ § ~

She is laughing now. It has taken her a year, but she has learned to laugh at the things she does not know. She laughs a lot. I love the sound of it, loud and almost ugly. Defiant.

The sound of pulling the knife away from the vein.

I survey the post-graduation scene through clear eyes, at portraits of families posing for photos beneath the overcast sky, royal blue popping in clusters on artificial green turf.

Mothers and fathers wipe wet eyes, wave at each other—survivors from the lifeboat they've shared for eighteen years—their jaws tightly forming smiles as they describe the end of the world in wistful giggles. *Things will never be the same. What will we do now?*

I can't believe it's all over.

I remove my sunglasses, even though the sky glares, honest and bright, over the delicate emotional chaos below. I wrap my arm around my second born who, released from marching band duties, has joined us at the sidelines. Her dark eyes sprout tiny tears of pride like a mother's might.

For her, this is a first-ever ending. Of course she will cry.

I point at the camera dangling from my oldest daughter's fingertips. "You're the graduate. You figure it out."

She squints at me, tears glossing her gorgeous long brown lashes. She does not laugh now. This is something she knows, that her peers—my peers—have yet to learn:

Today is not the end of the world.

And then, spying her best friend from water polo, she dives into the crowd without me, disappearing to take snapshots with her, with teachers and coaches and other friends, marking one life ended, another life started.

My eyes, when I look at my proud husband, remain clear and dry.

A Christmas Confession—Anonymous

We thought we were done with kids, but my wife and I ended up with our grandkids. Our daughter had a kid with an abusive drug addict. We can't really pass judgment on him, because she was a drug addict, too. The state took her son and we adopted him.

A year later, she had another drug-addicted baby. The hospital tested the baby for drugs, and a day later, my daughter's parental rights were revoked.

I was there every day when the baby went through withdrawals. My daughter and her boyfriend did not take the parenting classes, and did not complete the orders from the judge so we had to go through the adoption mess all over again. My wife and I swore we wouldn't go through this again, but we held that baby and couldn't turn him away. The baby was already calling us mom and dad.

~ § ~

A couple of years later, right after Thanksgiving, my employer laid everyone off. I was offered a crummier job for a pay cut, took it, and kept working. They changed our medical insurance and I had to pay more. I hunted for another job but didn't find anything that wouldn't require a move. Our legal requirements forbid us from moving out of state.

We were rolling into Christmas with no money. I "freed" a tree from the woods, and we decorated it with colored paper and pinecones. My wife was stressed, and so was I, but I pulled as many hours as I could to increase the size of my paycheck. It was still not enough.

In the mall was a Toys-for-Tots tree. They had toys perfect for my boys. I grabbed one, then another, and stuffed them in a backpack. I was hoping no one would notice.

I'm ashamed my kids had brand new toys from Santa that I stole, along with some dollar store toys. They were so happy Christmas morning, but I couldn't help feeling like shit. The toys I stole were their favorites.

Desert Daddy—Oren Hammerquist

As I step off the plane, I see the four women I care most about in the entire world. In the back of the group, tired and overworked, is my beautiful wife. In front of her are my three children; although far from being women yet, they are a year closer than they were when I saw them last.

Elisabeth, my youngest, is my best friend. She runs to hug me the second she sees me. Toddlers are always like that; they forgive you as soon as you come back. Well most toddlers are that way; her sister is an exception. Beth (my pet name for little Elisabeth) has been glued to me since the day she was born. For the part that I was there for anyway. I did the math on the plane as I flew across the Atlantic, and discovered I've seen less than fifty percent of her young life. When she was learning to crawl, she would get mad when I went to the bathroom. It's as if she knew I wouldn't be there in six months.

Rose is too tall now, but she seems to have forgiven me as well. In ten years, she'll resent me for far more than the two years of her life I missed. At five, she is in that stage where she talks too fast to be understood. Not that I mind at all, she can blabber on as long as she wants, even if I have no idea what princesses, airplanes, and school have to do with each other. Already, she trusts me more than her twin sister.

It may be hard to understand, but I hate video chatting. A psychiatrist might call this "transference." I blame an innocent party for those things I cannot control. A psychiatrist might be right too, but so often hearing them on the phone or on a computer screen only reminds you how far from home.

Since the day the twins were born, I have seen almost as much of them on my computer screen (in the few times I was lucky enough to have that option in the desert) as I have in the flesh. Between the twins and the toddler, I have seen first steps and heard first words, but not from the same child.

As I look up, I see Rose's twin, Anne, walking slowly towards me. She is coming to hug me, but only because she knows she is supposed to. Her sisters seem to think this situation is okay and she has caved to peer pressure. You can see in her eyes that she hasn't forgiven me yet.

I was prepared for this too, but only because of last time. It still stings. Five years, and I've been gone nearly half of that time. For some reason, my math skills are impeccable when it comes to my children. I barely passed math in college, but I can tell you exactly what proportion of my children's lives I have seen. "Serving my country" seems less altruistic and patriotic from the parent side, and feels like a meaningless platitude or excuse most of the time.

It has been three-and-a-half years since I came home the first time. I left my wife with two babies not even old enough to crawl. When I came back, they were walking and trying to talk. And still, at eighteen months, Anne was distant. I didn't know it back then. I had been home for six months when I noticed she was acting more like her sister. Anne was talking more, smiling and playing with me, and generally being a bubbly little girl.

"Have you noticed that Anne has been more outgoing recently?" I asked my wife.

"What do you mean?" she asked. When I explained the change in her behavior, my wife said, "She's always been like that."

Except not around me. Rose had immediately adjusted to my presence. That's the funny thing about twins, and it always surprises me. People tend to see how much they look alike and forget that they are so totally opposite. Even I am guilty of this.

"Just take your time, Anne. It's okay," I whisper to her so no one else can hear.

Sometimes, it is surprising to remember she is only ten minutes older than her sister and not ten months. Of course, the younger two will have their fights with me later (I'm expecting this from last time), but Anne has clearly reached the milestone first.

Parents always wonder if their kids understand, but the real question is whether you want them to. One year ago today, I called home from an airport on the other side of the country. I was about to cross the Atlantic (again) and it would be the last chance I had to talk to my kids for nearly two days because of flight time, jet lag, and bed times. Beth was too young, and Rose didn't know how to process my call.

It was Anne that asked me, "Why are you talking to me?" I tried to explain, but she simply didn't know all the words. When I finished, she asked, "But why are you talking to me?" again. She was too young to frame the question I knew she wanted to ask, "Why are you talking to me on the phone when you'll be home later today?"

At five, Anne understands more than she should. For Beth and Rose, they understand enough to be happy I am home. Anne understands that I was gone.

I love all of my children the same, but Anne is the one I worry about. It has been that way since the day she was born. Beth went home with us the day mommy did, and so did Rose. Anne was just shy of five pounds. Even now, she's shorter than her twin sister. She stayed in the hospital an extra week, has always had more trouble sleeping, and is the first in the house to get sick.

With Rose, I have to worry that she'll climb on something and jump off, that she'll fall down and scrape a knee, or she'll start a fight with a boy at school. (She already told me if a boy tried to kiss her she'd hit him, which made me explain things without laughing.) Beth is similar to Rose, but Anne is careful, methodical, and painfully shy. She wears her feelings on her shirt cuff. Of the three of them, she's the most like me, and so I worry. I know my own ability to hold a grudge, and if she's like me, it's going to be a while before we're okay in her eyes.

As we pile into the car, I buckle Beth into her car seat, but she is pouting. "I do it myself."

I'm confused by this, and my wife explains, "She can buckle her own belt now. She doesn't like it when you do it for her."

I stand outside the car with one child that resents me for leaving, one that will resent me later, and one that only wants to do things herself. A year is a very, very long time. Somewhere along the way, they grew up, and I missed it. My dad took business trips several times when I was young. In eighteen years, he was probably gone a total of six months or less. In five years, I've been gone half their lives. I have to admit I envy my father. He only had one kid to deal with and a boy at that. I have three girls pulling my heartstrings in different directions. A psychiatrist might say it is only natural that boys are closer to their mother, and girls are closer to their father. In my case, 'closer' to their father is ironic.

The only one in the family that has been here

before is my wife. She grew up in the first Gulf War with a father that spent more time in a desert (and in worse conditions) than her husband. She knows how it is to be away from your father for months and years at a time. She knows what it is like to move to a new city or country every two years. She's also the only one in the family who really knows the three children in the back seats. For every day I have missed being with them she has spent two with them. I wonder how she can keep from resenting me for fulfilling my duty to my country before my duty to her.

There is an old adage—maybe as empty as "duty, honor, country"—that says, "Absence makes the heart grow fonder." For a husband and wife, a homecoming is truly a magical thing—like a second honeymoon. For a toddler or baby, it is always overwhelming to see their daddy again. Unfortunately for me, the three behind me don't really understand why I'm back any more than they understood why I was gone in the first place.

The first day back is filled with awkward silences, cautious steps, and polite smiles. I have come to realize that it really doesn't matter what you expect when you come home, it will never be the same. Everyone has their own expectation of what will happen, and unlike last time, I have four ideas of my homecoming that are not mine.

I fill the awkward silence by trying to remember where the switches and buttons are in my car, and manage to run the windshield wipers by mistake while looking for the headlights. The car hasn't changed, but it still takes a while before I remember what to do. How much luck could I have with kids that went from toddler to school while I was gone? My children will catch me soon in years of life experience. They have already lived twelve years cumulatively, and I have just passed thirty. Each year they gain three years of experience and I fall two behind. Somewhere in high school— when I'm supposed to have all the answers— they'll have lived more than me. Except that every year I'm gone, I fall even further behind.

We head to the house because, after crossing the Atlantic (again), I need a shower as bad as I need those two and a half years back. In the front window, my wife has hung a sign saying "Welcome Home!" Everyone deals with the change in their own way. Optimism seems to be my wife's way, but cynicism has always been more natural to me. My children could no more read the sign than they could reach the window to hang it. I can't help but feel the irony of that statement with a five-year-old that won't trust me for weeks and a two-year-old that pouts because she doesn't want my help.

I am far more interested in the pictures that wallpaper our refrigerator. I look at them while Beth makes a game of bringing every stuffed animal from her room to me so I can see it. Some of the crayon pictures are carefully within the lines and have well-planned color schemes. These are Rose's. Even now, she has her mother's eye for color, and her mother's patience to get things right the first time. Anne's pictures are more typical of a small child that sees no point to coloring. Only one color was used (always pink), and lines are apparently optional. Near one side of the pictures, I see a Certificate of Participation with Anne's name on it. There is no matching one for Rose. Anne was recognized for her participation in a creative writing project in preschool. I'm not surprised; Anne has always impressed me with her vocabulary—often spouting words like "amulet." So like her father—whose favorite word at her age was "absolutely," and who used to write stories before he knew the alphabet. Still, I try to hide my disappointment that I missed this too.

Things are heading towards normal as the sun sets, but I'm still a year behind. There is no more high chair in our kitchen, and at dinner I realize my baby Beth doesn't use it any more. All three sit quietly sipping their soup from spoons. There is no huge mess from spilled food, and it hits me again how much I have missed. Rose has seconds on soup, but Anne has seconds on bread. Beth has seconds on everything, which doesn't surprise me. I knew she had gotten bigger, but I am shocked that she is nearly as tall as Anne. Both are shorter than Rose, who is past my hip now.

We watch TV, and it is comforting to know their tastes haven't changed. Anne sits next to me, but doesn't protest when Beth pushes her aside. Rose is still by best friend. Starting tomorrow, I know what is coming. No matter how much they change, all kids do the same thing on the second day. I have been gone a year, and they must test my boundaries. The problem is I don't really know where they are. My wife kept up day-to-day life when I was gone, and I don't know what might have changed since I crossed the Atlantic (again).

Beth has eight months of terrible twos to catch up on with daddy, but I have a feeling that, just like before, Anne will be the difficult one. Rose lacks subtlety, which makes her easier to deal with. You catch her breaking a rule, punish her, and the incident is over. Anne is, for lack of a better word, devious. When I tell Rose not to do something, Anne will do it to see what will happen. Clever and confusing. I can't punish her for something I told her sister not to do, but I can't let it go either. More difficult is the fact that while punishing Rose ends the problem, this is not the case with Anne. Anne mopes around leaving the recently absent father with the choice of cheering her up or letting her deal with it on her own.

I envy my parents once again having only one personality to deal with.

When bedtime comes, I am once again lost. All three can put their pajamas on by themselves, and while Beth needs help brushing her teeth, Rose and Anne really don't. They give me hugs and kisses, and I am relieved that at least something is still the same.

When I came back last time (after a year), Anne walked into our room to crawl in bed with mommy as she had been doing for the last few weeks. I told her it was okay then, but she gave me a look that showed confusion, anger, and sadness and went back to her bed. To this day, she has never come back to our room in the middle of the night. Anne and Rose are too old for that now, but Beth is confused by my sudden presence. I hear a sound in the early morning, and find her sleeping on the floor beside our bed. Once again, I have upset the normal routine without trying.

I pick her up, but now that she remembers her daddy, she wants to play. My wife deserves to sleep in after a year outnumbered by children, and I am jet lagged anyway. We move to the living room and I put on a cartoon while I turn on the computer.

It seems Beth is more forgiving than I realized and she helps me learn the routine. She is supposed to get a cup as soon as she gets up, and she makes sure I do this. When she is done, she lets me know she is supposed to have breakfast now. Typical of a girl who is growing way too fast, she isn't particular about what I make her; she eats it all the same.

I have two free days to make up for the last year, and then it's back to work. How will they understand? Every day when the twins come home from school at noon, will they assume I am gone for another year? I'm gone before

Beth wakes up most mornings. How will she process my absence? How many times will I have to relive my homecoming for better and worse?

If I fall two years behind the girls every year, then I must fall two days behind every night too. In a way, I feel like I can never really catch up. Do all parents feel that they are constantly trying to keep ahead of their children? Everything has changed in a year, and it is like there are nine people in my house now—the wife and three kids I left last year, the wife and three kids I came home to, and me. The only thing a desert daddy can hope for is to miss as little as possible.

Here Be Dragons—Andrea Lani

The lead singer of the band has blue eyes and blond hair that curls long and shaggy past his ears. His wiry body stands relaxed in jeans and a hooded sweatshirt. He sucks in his cheeks when he plays the guitar, his face an impassive mask of concentration, but once in a while one corner of his mouth lifts. When I catch his eye, I smile at him and he looks quickly away, as if he never saw me. I'll be taking him home after the show.

"Hello. Hello. Hello. Hello," he rasps into the microphone, a fair impression of Kurt Cobain. I smile again as he shrieks, "My libido!" and wonder if he looked the word up in the dictionary. I hope he just assumes it's a nonsense word to rhyme with "mosquito." My husband and I have been meaning to have The Talk with him, but haven't quite gotten around to it.

"How many of you like explosions?" he asks the crowd as his band, Double Jinx, launches into AC/DC's "TNT." My twelve-year-old child howls into the microphone, warning my fellow townspeople and me to lock up our daughters and wives. I know I should cringe at the misogynistic lyrics, but instead I pump my fist in the air and shout, "Oi! Oi!"

~ § ~

I had long ago given up worrying about the lyrics to the songs Milo plays. He started taking guitar lessons at nine, not long after that day in third grade when he came home from school and asked me if I had "ever heard of the Beatles?" My husband brought up an old *Meet the Beatles* album from his record collection in the basement and as Milo studied the cover and listened to the songs over and over during the next few weeks, I thought, what could be more wholesome than the music of the Fab Four with their pudding basin haircuts and boyish grins?

Once Milo moved on to later Beatles records, I convinced myself that "Lucy in the Sky with Diamonds" is no more about LSD than "Puff the Magic Dragon" is about pot. And when Milo's four-year-old brothers took up singing, "Why Don't We Do it in the Road?" I asked my husband, "What is that song even about?"

"What do you *think* it's about?" he replied, giving me *the* look.

"No, it can't possibly be about that," I said. "I mean, I can think of a thousand reasons why we wouldn't do *that* in the road."

When Milo came home from a guitar lesson having learned Johnny Cash's "Folsom Prison Blues," I asked, "What is your teacher doing teaching you these songs?"

"They're good songs, Mom," he replied.

He showed me how his guitar teacher had taught him to drop one of his fingers down a few frets as he strummed the chords, creating that classic Johnny Cash back-beat—dum-*dum*-dum.

"It makes it sound more interesting," he told me.

It was the music that drew Milo to the song, not the part about shooting a man in Reno. A few weeks later, he was learning the Rolling Stones' "Dead Flowers," and as he listened to the record, the stylus skipped, landing on the line about a needle and a spoon. *This song is about heroin,* I thought to myself. Not that there was any way Milo would know that—I'm not even sure how I knew it—*but really,* I wondered, *Is this an appropriate song for a nine-year-old?*

Not long after, as we drove home from a family outing to the beach, Milo belted out in the bluesiest voice his prepubescent vocal cords could muster, "I'm so lo-o-o-onely...," I wondered how he could possibly feel lonely, scrunched in the backseat between his two brothers as he sang about feeling suicidal and hating rock and roll. I could not fool myself into thinking that "Yer Blues" was sweet and innocent and tried to figure out how to explain suicide to a nine-year-old and steer him away from that particular tune when I heard one of his brothers say, "You hate rock and roll!"

"No, I don't," said Milo.

"*He* does," replied his brother, "the guy who's singing."

"John Lennon doesn't hate rock and roll," Milo explained. "The person who's telling the story does."

After that, I relaxed. If Milo's thinking was sophisticated enough to differentiate between writer and narrator, then I probably wouldn't have to worry about him being unduly influenced by his favorite songs. And, as he pointed out, they *are* good songs. As a writer with no musical background, I connect most deeply with a song's lyrics. I listen carefully to the words, turning them over in my mind like handfuls of colored pebbles. I am as impatient with nonsense as I am with excessively simplistic or cliché language. The music is, for me, secondary. I approach it with a Duke Ellington, "If it sounds good, it is good," attitude, without further analysis. Milo is a musician, and murder, suicide, drugs, and sex are secondary, or perhaps even immaterial, to the sounds his hands coax from the strings.

~ § ~

Over the three years of his guitar playing, Milo has moved from the Beatles into the realms of hard rock and heavy metal, the music I avoided at his age. The kids who listened to that kind of music—the ones who wore ripped Levi's, jeans jackets, black high-tops, and Megadeath t-shirts, who feathered their hair and clustered in the alley I had to walk through on my way home from school—we called "stoners." At the time, I had no idea what that term referred to, and now, looking back as a mother of a seventh-grader, I have a hard time imagining kids that age smoking pot. Perhaps I was judgmental then, or perhaps I am naïve now. In any case, their taste in music and style of dress marked them as different from me and my Duran Duran-listening friends.

Those kids appeared to me as angry, surly dropouts from the normal society of good grades and homework and watching "Who's the Boss?" on TV, and I associated their music with cigarettes and drugs and rebelliousness. But my kid is as different from those classmates—or how I perceived those classmates—as I can imagine. He doesn't show any propensity for wearing black, other than his favorite Van Halen t-shirt. He gets mostly A's in school, plays trumpet in band, plays forward on the soccer team, and pitches for his Little League team. He is warm and affectionate, folding his lengthening body into my lap to cuddle as we watch "Jeeves and Wooster" DVDs. He gets along with most of the kids in his class and his rebelliousness extends to resisting when I encourage him to sign up for Junior Honor Society.

Now, as an adult, I can listen to the music favored by those *other* kids with a different ear. While I still don't exactly love hard rock, I can listen to Queen, Pink Floyd, or even Quiet Riot with appreciation for the pleasure the music brings my son. I also try to figure out why I hated this music when I was Milo's age, why I preferred British pop and new wave. In part I think my preference goes back to the lyrics— words I could comprehend, about love, broken hearts, or, sometimes, politics, sung in voices that were tender, not harsh or angry, to music either upbeat or sad, but not abrasive. I have to admit the pretty boys singing on MTV, with their fluffy hair, pouty lips, and melty eyes, had something to do with it. Also, I never really liked guitar riffs and solos, until I heard them played by my own kid.

Now, when I'm driving in my car and get bored with my alternative radio station or NPR, I switch to the hard rock station. I find myself hearing "Enter Sandman" run through my mind when I can't sleep at four in the morning or humming "Rock 'n' Roll Ain't Noise Pollution" in my cubicle at work.

Despite his hard-rock leanings, the songs Milo and his band perform seem fairly mild in content, nothing too overtly sexual or drug-related (if we ignore the implied raping and pillaging in "TNT"). Other than the murder tune "Black Blood," the songs he writes are humorous and wholesome, about pizza and foursquare and old Volvos. I no longer ask him what he thinks a song is about. Perhaps, after he told me he thought The Eagles' "Life in the Fast Lane" was about driving on the highway, I believed his innocence—and literal mind— would inoculate him against sex and drugs and early death in music, and in life.

A conversation he and I had other day reinforced this notion. Milo said to me, "It is my belief that AC/DC's lyrics are a bad influence on people's lyric-writing abilities because they mostly write about bad stuff."

"Like what?" I asked.

"Evil, guns, explosions, hell, rock and roll." He laughed. "Just kidding. Rock and roll's not bad."

"So will you stop listening to them?"

"No. I still love AC/DC, but I've gotten over my dark lyric phase. Now I'm more influenced by Frank Zappa and Weird Al to write goofy songs."

As Double Jinx plays the opening bars in on The Ramones' "Blitzkrieg Bop" and my body starts bouncing around to a rhythm it understands, I realize there is another reason I never gravitated toward hard rock when I was young: I like music I can dance to. During my first two years of high school, I went out dancing almost every weekend with four of my friends. At first, we went to FunPlex, a big mall-like structure in the suburbs of Denver that held bowling alleys, arcades, and a roller-skating rink that turned into an underage dance floor on Friday and Saturday nights. We would gather at one of my friends' houses in the afternoon to tease and spray our hair and try on a dozen different outfits before one of our parents shuttled us to the club, where we spun right 'round to Dead or Alive and safety danced with Men Without Hats. After a while, we graduated to INXS, a club with dark rooms that pulsed strobe lights and blasted New Order and

The Cure, and hallways that smelled like the Clove cigarettes smoked by boys dressed all in black.

As high school wore on, I got more involved with other friends, and all four of the girls in my dance club circle ended up dropping out of school and running away from home. They weren't bad kids, and our dance club nights were pretty innocent, not counting that one time we snuck Jack Daniels into the FunPlex bathroom inside a mini Finesse hairspray bottle. I don't remember the details of that time in my friends' lives, other than stories of heavy drinking and intense involvement with boys. I was too young, too sheltered, and too self-involved to recognize whatever troubles played into their cascade of life events.

As I contemplate my child's future and his choice of music, I find I conflate adolescence and rock and roll. In my mind they lie beyond the uncharted and dangerous territories labeled, "Here be dragons," on an ancient map.

I wonder if I've inherited a cultural bias, handed down from my grandparents' generation, or if I genuinely have something to fear. Falling on the "rational fear" side, adolescents have the highest rates of avoidable deaths due to accidents, suicide, drugs, and weapon injuries.

For the most part, my own teenage years land in the "unfounded fear" column. Although I clashed with my parents, I got good grades, worked summer jobs, served on student council, and swam on the swim team. But episodes of heavy drinking loom large in my memory—parties at friends' houses, that first time I got drunk on peppermint schnapps and hot chocolate in the parking lot of Red Rocks before a Howard Jones concert when I was thirteen, and the next year, discovering I had a proclivity for downing shots of tequila outside a U2 concert. It doesn't escape my attention that rock concerts set the stage for my early drinking forays. It frightens me to think how vulnerable I was in those situations and how lucky I was that no one took advantage of my vulnerability. It frightens me to imagine the situations my son might find himself in, without even being aware of the dangers.

The rock stars themselves flash in red lights: "rational fear." In an effort to bend a school assignment theme of "healthy living" toward his interests, Milo and I look up "musicians who died of drugs" on Wikipedia. At first I'm surprised by how few there are, or at least how few I recognize—Jimi Hendrix, Janis Joplin, Jim Morrison, Gram Parsons, Elvis Presley, Keith Moon, Sid Vicious. *Surely,* I think, *Many more rock stars* haven't *died of drug overdoses.* Milo adds Bon Scott, dead of alcohol poisoning, to the list, and Kurt Cobain, whose suicide was preceded by struggles with heroin addiction. Later I click on a link to "deaths in rock and roll" and as I scroll down the list of car and plane crashes, drug overdoses, murders, suicides, alcohol poisonings, falls from buildings and bridges, electrocutions by their own equipment, HIV-related complications, and heart attacks, strokes, and liver and kidney failures that I suspect may trace their origins to booze and drugs, "rock star" looks as dangerous a profession as "coal miner." I notice, too, that the vast majority of the untimely dead are male.

I don't honestly expect my son to become a rock star, but substance abuse and early death are not the exclusive domain of the famous, and when a talented young musician from the local music scene was found dead in his apartment a couple of years ago, I thought seriously about whether it was wise to encourage Milo to continue on the path of rock and roll. I still wonder if time spent playing guitar, writing songs, and mixing tunes on the computer will keep him out of the kinds of trouble brought on by boredom and lack of purpose, or if music will expose him to people and situations that can destroy a life. For now I'm counting on his ability to separate writer from narrator to translate into separating music from musician, to emulate talent while eschewing vice.

I also think about what kept me on a straight-and-narrow path when my friends' lives went astray, and the most significant difference I can come up with is that I had a stable home life.

But I cannot take for granted that my husband's and my loving presence in our son's life will keep him safe. His peer groups, his changing adolescent brain, the circumstances he will find himself in, all will play a role in how Milo's teenage years play out. These other influences—unknown and outside of my control—scare me the most.

Not long after Milo's first performance, I took him to see his guitar teacher play in a CD release concert. The singer thanked his parents at the beginning of the show and even said, "Sorry, Mom," after singing a lyric about drowning in his own shit. The love songs he dedicated to his wife, which is, of course, how it should be. Back when Milo was still in his Beatles phase, he held open a songbook to "All My Lovin'," and, as we sang together, I felt the rift that divides us as mother and son more acutely than I ever had before—him too young to even imagine loving someone so intensely that you can't be parted, and me old enough that I barely remember that feeling.

It is the sweet sorrow of parenting that we put all our love and attention into these little beings, and our success is defined by their leaving. If we do our job right, our children will thank us from their life's stage, but their love songs will be sung to someone else. It shocked me recently, when I realized I am raising not a child, but a future adult. I'm thankful for the eighteen-year gestation period of the man that leaves me free to focus on the child in the moment, with only occasional glimpses into the future—imagining the terrible toddler in my sweet baby, the schoolboy in my three-year-old, and the man in the twelve-year-old sitting next to me. As we watched his guitar teacher perform, I could see it as if it were happening in that moment, Milo on stage, taller than I am, a day's growth of whiskers coarsening his face, singing songs that delve into realms that should be hidden from a mother's view, and dedicated to a woman who is not me.

I glanced at my son, his still-smooth face that impassive mask, his blue eyes riveted, taking in every movement of fingers on frets onstage, and

I could feel time moving by so fast, launching my child into the future. Then his hand went to his mouth and wiggled the loose bicuspid he'd been worrying for days. My glimpse into the future faded and I relaxed. He was still my twelve-year-old boy; we still had time.

~ § ~

Double Jinx kicks into a song they wrote themselves. "Black blood spattered on the ceiling. Black blood gives a bad feeling. Black blood broke down the door. Black blood all over…the floor." This is Milo's first rock performance, and it's as different as I can imagine from his first time on stage, at his preschool holiday concert, where he sat with his hands clasped and his lips clamped together, as if he were afraid he might accidentally start singing "Jingle Bells" if he opened his mouth. On the way to the show I asked him if he was nervous, and he replied, "No, I've played onstage before," referring, I assumed, to the time he played guitar at a school assembly, or the two band concerts he's played trumpet in.

The bass thumps. Milo shreds his guitar solo. The crowd—friends and neighbors out enjoying our town's annual celebration—goes wild. Over the next few months Milo and his best friend, the bassist, will play twice in a local pub and at a multi-band show called *Rock, Shock, and Metal: The Loud and Obnoxious Concert.* They will borrow adult drummers from other bands, use equipment that blows their little amps away, and even play under colored, spinning lights in the smoky-bar haze left by a fog machine. Each time I will be astounded at the self-confidence and poise of my child, standing onstage, singing, joking with the audience, his fingers flashing over the strings of his guitar.

I want to freeze this moment—my blue-eyed boy onstage, singing and playing and banging his shaggy blond head—as I have a million other moments over the last twelve years. My son stands on a precipice, childhood behind him, adolescence ahead. It's a frightening, uncharted land, and I'm not sure I'm ready to tread there. I don't know where Milo will take his music, or where music will lead him. A mother's fears lie in that uncharted territory. But so do my hopes that my love and Milo's level head will carry him through the teenage years unscathed. For now, though, I set aside the future and bask in the present—my son leaning into the microphone as he closes out the set and says, "That's Double Jinx."

Night Owls—Stephanie Vanderslice

Memories of my sons' childhoods wax and wane in their clarity. Some swaths of time have vanished completely. I still remember nights in the hospital after Will, my second and last child was born. Sleep was elusive then, not because Will was rooming in with me, although he was, or because he was particularly fussy, because he wasn't, but because hospitals aren't ideal places to get a lot of rest. There's always a light on somewhere, a nurse coming in to fiddle with your IV or ask your name, rank and serial number, since actually *being* who you think you are seems to be a critical sign of recovery.

With the flurry of visitors during the day, the steady stream of family, friends, pediatricians, lactation consultants, and cafeteria quality assurance emissaries (no lie), it was only after visiting hours had long passed and the moon had risen over the black tar parking lot of St. Vincent's Doctor's Hospital that I had time alone with my new son.

I remember savoring the quiet in the semi-dark while Will lay swaddled beside me in the bassinet, sleeping with the faintest suggestion of a smile on his face, his tiny starfish hands fisted under his chin. I remember the silky-smooth curve of his forehead, the way his pink lips pursed into a perfect bow.

Fortunately, Will was a placid, easy baby in those first few days, content to eat, mostly, and make faces in his sleep. I was determined he would room with me in the hospital whether he was "easy" or not. Four years earlier, when his brother, Jackson, had been born in Louisiana, "rooming in" was decidedly frowned upon. Mother's needed their rest after a baby was born, so it was recommended the baby be left in the nursery and brought to her for feedings. Inexperienced and eager to please, we let

Jackson sleep in the nursery.

The first night we brought Jackson home from the hospital, however, he gagged and spit up mucus on and off for hours. The sounds were horrific to this new mother's ears and I didn't sleep a wink in between changing the sheets of his bassinet as he soaked them through with saliva and mucous, and growing more and more frantic that he would choke. Still, he slept on, unperturbed by his coughing and gasping, as I became more certain that if I'd only had him room with me at the hospital I would know whether this was typical or not. When morning came, he was fine and though I steeled myself for a repeat the next night, his sleep was quiet and restful and his sheets dry. Never again, I swore, with the fervor only a new parent can muster. My next baby would room in.

My mother used to call Will my "little shadow." When he was a toddler I couldn't so much as go to the bathroom by myself without him standing outside the door plaintively calling my name. By contrast, Jackson was always the independent one, the one who didn't like holding hands, the one who marched off to preschool without so much as a backwards glance, leaving me standing in the hallway holding a yellow school bus-shaped backpack in one hand and a sack lunch in the other, mouth agape, wondering what had just happened.

His teacher, Mrs. Patty just smiled. "Oh honey," she said, "It's better this way, believe me. This is a *good* thing."

And so it went. Ten years later, when we dropped Jackson at a summer academic camp nine hours away, we sat through a lengthy parent orientation where we were continually reminded that this was probably the first time our campers had been away from home for an extended period and they were sure to be homesick. *Gravely* homesick. My eyes filled with tears and a dry knot tightened across my chest. They were right. Jackson had never been so far away from home before, for such a length of time. Even an independent streak as strong as his might waver under these conditions.

Afterwards, we found him in the dorm lounge

for our last goodbye. I was determined to be brave. I hugged his skinny frame tight and opened my mouth to let out the litany of encouraging farewells I had been preparing for this transition.

"Bye then," he said, pivoting blithely on his heels with a little wave. "I'm going to play some foosball." Again, I stood there, mouth agape, wondering what had just happened.

It wasn't until Will started nursery school that Mrs. Patty's words began to resonate, in the vise-like grip of his little hands every morning as we crossed the threshold of his classroom, where Mrs. Ruth would guide us through our daily separation ritual. There was the first, "Don't go, Mommy," at the cubicles, and then the request for "one more hug," and then, "one more," followed by the inevitable attempts at distraction, "Look Will, Carlos and Timmy are making a city with blocks. Don't you want to join them?" Then finally Mrs. Ruth's reassuring, "He'll be fine once you leave. He always is."

Transitions were always a struggle, whether it

was taking Will to school, leaving him with a babysitter or sitting on the sofa holding his four-year-old self in my arms and explaining why I had to go on one of my infrequent business trips.

"But I just want you to stay home," he'd sniff. "I just want you to stay with *me*."

Once I'd said good-bye, I'd enter into my own psychic battle not to cancel my trip. After all, what was the worst that would happen if I got someone to present this paper for me—just this once?

Career wise, probably nothing would happen, I knew. But I also knew all too well, as someone whose own mother had removed her from St. Gregory's Nursery School because I likewise struggled with transitions, the frantic feeling deep down that if I just cried desperately enough, I might get to stay home. I had never gotten over it. Much as I wanted to give in to *my* baby, I just couldn't bear to set that pattern in motion.

Looking through my gratitude journal from

that time, I find a description of my return from that trip: "Will: Let's hug each other 100 times!"

It's almost painful to read.

Over the years, my husband and I have grown accustomed to hearing, again and again, how, as one friend exclaimed upon meeting our sons for the first time, "Wow! You certainly split the gene pool right down the middle." In fact, the extent to which we hear that phrase probably rivals "Vanderslice? How do you spell that?— pause—Oh. Just like it sounds!"

But really, it is rather uncanny, the way Jackson favors his father and the Vanderslice line, with his lush, curly dark hair, luminous peridot eyes, and strong bone structure, while Will favors me and my side of the family, with his Germanic coloring, his shiny-straight dark blonde hair, and sparkling, indigo eyes. Just for fun, I once showed a friend a photo of myself as a toddler and her first question was, "Why is Will wearing a dress?"

As most parents do, I like to think I love both

my children equally, though perhaps differently. I adore Jackson; he is my sweet, kind, brilliant, first born, the child I longed and prayed for, the first man I fell in love after my husband. I would be lying if I didn't admit I enjoyed having my own little "mini-me," in the form of this cherub-faced child who actually *liked* holding my hand and who clearly needed me in ways his older brother had not.

In fact, during his preschool and elementary years, Will's need was such that he fought to sleep with us almost every night, a battle he rarely won because it usually resulted in my husband curled unhappily on the sofa or the floor. He did manage to prevail on road trips, however. We'd scarcely roll our luggage past the double beds in our motel room when Will would announce triumphantly, "Daddy can sleep with Jackson and Mommy can sleep with ME!"

"Jeez, he's not too Oedipal is he?" my friend, Hannah, who is also a clinical therapist, once observed wryly.

The compromise that ultimately preserved my marriage was that Will and I would cuddle up in his bed each night and I'd read to him, starting with *Frog and Toad* and *Bedtime for Frances* and progressing through the years to *Harry Potter* before eventually, we turned to reading side by side, together. Once he fell asleep, I delicately removed myself and tiptoed downstairs.

I didn't really mind. It was nice to feel needed, and Will and I really "got" each other during those years. We sighed together over the adventures of the forlorn porcelain rabbit in *The Miraculous Journey of Edward Tulane* and laughed at some of the more unintentionally ridiculous scenes in *Swiss Family Robinson* (especially the ones that featured ostriches, boa constrictors and antelope, not to mention the occasional boar, lion, and whale, all inhabiting one island). While his brother slept in the bunk above us and his father slept on the first floor below us, we two night owls de-constructed the daily intricacies of third grade and contemplated age-old questions like, "Mommy, who told us the name of the world?"

One night, somewhere along in middle school, while we were each reading our own books side by side, Will reached over and clutched my shoulders.

"What is it?" I was certain something he'd been reading had frightened him.

"It's just so hard, Mommy," he said, drawing back and looking at me, his eyes bright with tears and confusion.

"What is?" I asked.

"Growing up," he said plainly.

"I know, sweetie," I told him, helpless to find other words. "I know."

All this time I knew too, that in the normal scheme of things, I was going to lose my little shadow. But knowing never makes it any easier when it happens. About a year after he had confessed to me the pain of growing up, Will told me I took up too much room in his full-sized bed and that he would prefer to read alone.

"Well, that could have gone worse," I remember thinking. In a way, I was glad to get my evenings back, to not have my own bedtime dictated by when my son finally gave in to sleep.

But that was just the beginning. In the months that followed, Will unfurled an animosity toward me that seemed in direct and opposite proportion to how close we'd been.

On the surface, it seemed completely arbitrary. I knew it wasn't.

Suddenly the child who had clutched me like a life raft in a swirling sea recoiled at the slightest touch: my hand on his shoulder, a pat on the back. Suddenly, when it was time to say goodbye before a business trip, Will would just shrug, barely looking at me. I was leaving. *So?*

And then one day, as I was dropping him off at school with the usual morning pleasantries, "Have great day sweetie. I love you..."

"Well I *don't* love you," snarled my former

shadow, apropos of nothing. No argument that morning, no building tension, none that I was aware of, anyway.

"Do you have to say that *every* morning," he continued as the hum of our Toyota compensated for my stricken silence. "And stop calling me sweetie. I *hate* it when you call me sweetie."

Sweetie was a particular term of endearment between mothers and children in my family, initiated, as far as I knew, by my mother's mother. She called all of her ten grandchildren sweetie, always with her musical Irish lilt.

Sweetie was just what you said to show you loved someone.

Hoping Will's behavior was a fluke, a sort of one-off anomaly, like the time I took an antihistamine when I was still nursing him and he turned into the Tasmanian Devil, I ignored it. For the next several days, I persisted with my cheerful morning farewells, each time meeting the same response.

"Well, I still love you," I said one morning, "even if you're really hurting my feelings right now. And I don't think I can stop telling you that. But I will stop calling you sweetie, if that's what you want."

After searching for a less offensive alternative, I finally settled upon "handsome" and Will accepted this, beginning an uneasy truce. The following year, he walked to the junior high, a few blocks from our house. I got used to life without my shadow.

~ § ~

Late one January night, it had been snowing for a few hours, the flakes falling in a steady stream under the triangle of the streetlight, growing brighter against the rising moon. The house was quiet and I thought I was the only one awake when Will appeared in the living room, staring out the front window into the night.

"Look at it come down," he said, gazing out into the night. Snow is just rare enough to be cherished in our part of Arkansas.

And so, framed by the doorway, my son pulled a coat and boots on over his pajamas as if in a trance. Snow, the great equalizer, had demolished the stigma of leaving the house in anything other than black t-shirts with crumbling rock band decals and gray skinny jeans.

I stood at the window and watched as he tilted his head under an inky sky swirled with faint pink clouds and held his tongue out to catch the flakes.

Next, he a path around the yard, making designs in the snow with his boots, and an enormous heart emerged, with initials inside. He had a girlfriend now, his first real girlfriend. I knew whose initials those were.

I stepped out onto the porch to risk a suggestion. "You should take a photo of it and send it to her."

He turned around, nodding. "That's what I was thinking," he said, passing me, remarkably unscowling, on the way inside to get his phone.

He returned and I watched him again, moving around the porch, trying to catch the heart from different angles. Finally, he paused over the phone, his fingers a flurry of movement.

"Did you send it to her?"

He nodded.

"Can I see it?"

He flashed the camera towards me for an instant; I had to be quick to catch a glimpse. Then he looked down at the image himself, a faint self-satisfied grin playing over his lips.

As I watched him smile to himself in half-light like I had so many years ago, I touched his shoulder. Lost in his own thoughts, he didn't flinch or pull away but let it rest there. Inside, his father and brother slept on. Tomorrow, they would awaken to a bright, white world long before we would, but for the moment it was just the two of us, together again, and for now that would have to be enough.

Have a Cigar—Michael Schofield

January First has been out now for over two weeks. Thanks to all of you, it just recorded its second week on the New York Times Combined (electronic and hardcover) Bestseller's List, something I never expected.

So I am getting a lot of people telling me "Congratulations."

I know people mean well. They say it out of common courtesy. I get that. But it's difficult for me to respond. I have to respond. These are people who bought and read the book. Their purchase has put me one step closer to securing Jani and Bodhi's future after I am dead and gone.

Online it is easier. I can just type "Thank you" and move on. That's the nice thing about the online world. You can kill the conversation whenever you want. Recently, I wished one of my Facebook friends "Happy birthday." She responded to my single line on her wall by expressing wonder that now that I was a "celebrity" I still took the time to wish people a happy birthday.

I know she meant well. She's a nice person. But I could not think of a nice way to respond to that, so I didn't.

I get that for most Americans, and perhaps the rest of the world, TV appearances and getting a book published equal "celebrity." Except that I hate the term. It implies that I am a different person than I was before. But I was a different person long before anyone in the public knew my name or Jani's name. It was the experiences within the book that made me a different person, not the book itself. The fact that I can go into a Barnes & Noble and open a book to see myself on the back flap doesn't change me.

"Congratulations."

It doesn't quite work.

Congratulations for what?

What exactly is it that I did?

"Thank you for being so honest."

What else would I do? Hide that my daughter has schizophrenia? Kinda hard to do when every aspect of my life is totally defined by Jani (and Bodhi). I have no life beyond them. There is nothing left of whoever I was before Jani became ill.

"It's so great you stood by Jani."

She's my daughter. I brought her into this world. What was I supposed to do?

"You could have sent her away."

What would be the point in doing that? Like I told you, "my" life was already gone. Okay, so let's say I send Jani away. Then what? Go on with my life? What life?

"You could have run away."

I tried that a couple of times. The first time I tried to run away had to be cut from the book for length reasons but it is in the blog "Stay Together for the Kids." The second was the ultimate escape attempt, which is recorded in the book. I didn't run away because I am more noble or better than any of you. I didn't run away because the Universe or God or whatever you want to call it wouldn't let me. The first time It wouldn't let me by scaring off the other woman (see "Stay Together for the Kids"). The second time... Well, the second time It directly intervened. And did. It had to. What are the odds that Jani would walk into the kitchen and speak to me as I about to swallow a second mouthful of anti-depressants? I didn't save her life. It was the other way around. How many more pills would it have taken to kill me on that June day in 2009? Was that final, lethal pill waiting in the next swallow? Would I have kept going? Would I have vomited all over the kitchen floor? Gone into a seizure? Foamed at the mouth?

Did you know most suicide victims never

leave a note? It's true. Only a small minority ever do. Interestingly enough, those few suicide notes are rarely an explanation. You want to know what the most common opening line in a suicide note is?

"I'm sorry."

These people are about to kill themselves and they are writing an apology.

Why? If they know they are going to hurt those they leave behind, why do they do it?

Because it's a mental illness. It's called severe depression. You know what you are doing is wrong but you can't help it.

I believe in God. When I drove away that day to die, God spoke to me.

No, no apparition appeared to me in the middle the road. No booming voice from a burning bush spoke to me.

It was a very quiet voice, inside my head, in the same voice all my internal thoughts are in.

"You can't do this."

It wasn't a command. It wasn't said with desperation. It stated as a quiet fact, as if I was simply prolonging the inevitable. It knew I wasn't really going to kill myself, that I could not just abandon Jani, Bodhi, and Susan to whatever life might throw at them. So why I was pretending like this? This was just a charade, me having a tantrum and raging at the Universe because I couldn't "save" Jani.

And It was right. I was just playing at trying to run away. Because there was no running away. This is Jani's life. This is Bodhi's life. This is Susan's life. This is my life.

I had a job to do, even if I sucked at it.

Never assume that your "calling" will be something that you're good at. God, Nature, Universe, Allah, whatever you call It, doesn't call you to work because you are good at the job. It calls you because It knows you will persevere. It calls you because It knows that in those moments where you feel like you are going to give up… you don't. It calls you because It knows that if you go over the edge, you're gonna catch that branch or jagged rock just underneath. Yeah, you might cut yourself to pieces but you will hang on rather than let go. You will live with the pain of what you have done rather than let go and fall to your death. You will break every bone in your damn body. It will let you lay there for awhile, feeling sorry for yourself. But in the end It knows what you know. You aren't just gonna lie there forever. You are going to roll over and crawl your way back.

Because you've got a job to do.

What is that job?

It's very simple.

Stay alive.

That's all It needs you to do. Stay alive.

~ § ~

You have to stay alive because one day you will be called upon to help someone else stay alive and you will be the ONLY person who can do that. And they in turn will be called upon to help someone else stay alive so that they in turn can help someone else stay alive.

That is how you change the world. You stay alive.

I don't deserve congratulations for writing a book or being on TV. The only thing I did was stay alive. And by staying alive, I help to keep Jani alive.

And she in turn helps so many of you to stay alive. I know this because you've told me.

And in turn you will help others to stay alive.

That is it. That is the noblest thing you can do, the highest calling of a human being. Survive. Even if today, yesterday, last week, last month, last year, or your entire life has been one big pile of shit, you have to stay alive. Your life has value. You keep others alive.

That is also why suicides tend to happen in sets. It's a chain reaction. You fall and the whole chain crumbles without you.

If there is one thing I have learned through all

of this, it is that EVERY SINGLE life has value.

So please stop congratulating me. You can congratulate Jani because she has earned it. She has fought back from a 50/50 prognosis to odds I'd take to Vegas if I could go to Vegas.

But I what I really want you to do is congratulate yourself for being alive tonight. And then I want to find another human being and congratulate them on being alive. And tell them to do the same.

We're all part of this chain.

And I am hoping that the next time I hear "congratulations" it will be from somebody who's never heard of me.

To My Fat, Lazy, Geeky Son— Anonymous

You know I love you, kiddo. Being your Father has made me happier than anything in the world. I would do anything for you...but I have some things I have to get off my chest.

You're sitting there playing Minecraft on a summer day. Your fat is poking out of your shirt. Your pudgy feet are on the coffee table. Your only friend in the real world is a creepy kid who wears a winter coat even in summer. You have no ambition. No curiosity. No interest in books, or music. No interest in the mechanical. No interest in going outside. Your grades are terrible, and every single day I feel like I failed you as a Dad.

When I drag you off the couch, you do it. You don't talk back, and that's good, at least. Still, as we go out and do something you follow along with no expression on your face. I point out something exciting and interesting, and you couldn't care less. You're afraid of heights. Afraid of fast rides at amusement parks. You break down in tears whenever you're upset.

You're spoiled. This summer you went to space camp. A week at the beach. Two weeks at summer camps with your creepy friend. I grew up too poor for any of that sort of thing. You have it all...yet when you return, you just shrug and tell me all the bad parts of the experience.

I try to eat healthy around you, but as soon as you go back to your Mom's, it's all fast food and sitting around. I'm glad you're starting to get into Tae Kwon Do, but I failed you by not pushing you into team sports earlier. I hated my Dad for making me play baseball, and I didn't want you to go through that.

Every time you break down in tears, I want to

punch you and give you something to really cry about. I never would, and perhaps that's my own weakness. This world doesn't have room for a man who cries or who can't handle emergencies.

Perhaps you'll turn it around. At 13, I was pretty geeky myself. I loved comic books. The video arcades. My action figures. But even then I was still active. I rode my bike over to my friend's house. We built forts. Raced dirt bikes. Blew things up and got into trouble. At your age I had been brought home by the police twice. I couldn't imagine you breaking into a place to steal beer to impress a girl you liked.

I'm sorry that I've been too soft with you. I'm sorry that I loved you too much to make you tough enough for the coming years. I'm sorry that I didn't push you harder in many areas.

I'm also sorry that I'll never tell you these things in person, or let you know about it. As you get older and seek the validation from your Father, in a story as old as time, I feel like that disappointment in you will always be there as a gulf that can't be crossed. I still love you, my son. I just wish I had been a better man.

Life Just Keeps Getting Worse—Anonymous

I am a single mom of a wonderful son.

My son was arrested for 1st degree murder. He was 19, and never in trouble with the law. He has a mental illness and was diagnosed with bipolar and Borderline Personality Disorder (BPD). I am not offering this as an excuse or for sympathy, but to explain why he made bad choices. He has trouble with his emotions and poor social skills, and is at high risk for becoming a victim inside prison. I worry he will have a difficult time keeping himself safe, and doubt my son will last more than a few years in incarceration.

The details in this story have been changed

because my son's arrest made the national news. I feel wary of being identified, judged, and criticized. I am terrified for him, and don't want to jeopardize his future by saying something wrong, or revealing something I shouldn't.

~ § ~

A few months ago, my day began like most days, getting ready for work. I dropped my son off at his job and then went to mine. He said he would get a ride home that afternoon.

When it was dark and he wasn't home yet, I wasn't worried because he texted me that he was with friends. He said he'd be home later.

~ § ~

I got a call in the middle of the night from the police station. My son said, "Mom, I've been arrested."
I thought he was playing a joke on me.

"For what?" I asked.

He couldn't say. He told me he had to go,

and to 'please post bail.' The police got on the phone but couldn't tell me what happened because my son was an adult. They told me I could come and get his belongings at the police station. I don't know how I drove to the station. I was in such a panic. When I got there I was frantic. No one would tell me anything. I had to sign for a long list of belongings that I took home. Some of the things I didn't recognize. The police refused to give me a copy of what I had signed for.

Over the next few days, I reached out to family and called his friends to try to piece the puzzle together. After a few days, the bail was lowered enough so that we could afford to get him out.

When I picked him up at the jail, he ran to my car, hugged me and just sobbed for a few minutes. It broke my heart to see him like that. Over the next few days, he told me how he didn't see the consequences of what he had done. He regretted everything and was sorry. He became fearful of going outside. He lost his job, and could only return to work pending a positive outcome of the trial.

Seven days later, I received a phone call at work from a detective looking for my son. They told me they were outside my home with a search warrant. I asked them to wait to enter until I got there, because I wanted to see the warrant.

I left work immediately, but because of traffic, it took me a long time to get home. As I approached my street, I found the road was closed. Police cars, helicopters, and a swat team descended on my home. I was told the FBI was involved. I later learned several snipers waited at the basement back entrance, told to shoot if they saw my son trying to exit.

When I stopped to ask a police officer what was going on, they demanded I get out of my car. They searched me and forced into the back of a police cruiser. Two officers led me to the local police station where I waited for over an hour, crying and terrified, until the FBI agents came to interrogate me.

Since that day, I have been unable to return

to my home. It was declared unsafe for occupancy, and everything in it was destroyed and put into a biohazard landfill. I would not be reimbursed for the destruction of my belongings, and was charged over $40K for their services. I am now homeless and facing bankruptcy.

I have amazing friends who have given me a shoulder to cry on, food and clothing, and a place to stay. My parents and extended family have shunned me because of what happened.

I struggle to understand why this happened. From what little I know, my son did a very stupid thing out of a broken heart and severe depression. I ask myself everyday why I couldn't prevent it. If only I could have gotten him help from someone he trusted. If only he had been able to start his new job. If only he hadn't met that girl. If only I'd been a better mom. There are still so many regrets and unanswered questions, and the "what ifs" have led me to a circle of pain. The "what ifs" have stolen my mind and emptied my soul.

I love my son, but I hate what he did. I hate the fact that his father and I passed along genes for severe depression and anxiety. I blame myself. I feel very empty, very alone. I don't know if I can ever heal from this.

My son has a life sentence. The victim's friends and family were angry, feeling he should have been put to death. I am truly sorry to the victims, my community, and the world. I cannot go back and undo anything, or prevent my son from committing this terrible crime.

I am still in turmoil as every day something new happens, and it's usually not good news. I wouldn't believe all of this if someone had told me the story. It seems to just keep getting worse.

I hope I will survive with my mind and heart intact. My heartache is fresh and goes very deep, and my only hope is that the world will offer compassion.

The Write Mother—
Rebecca T. Dickinson

Blood from a man's brain splattered on his shattered windshield. He drove his car into a house. The man had alcohol in his blood. A paramedic put her hand over my camera lenses and told me not to photograph the victim. I stood behind the yellow tape, as always, and did my job with the professionalism she performed hers. The EMS worker and I crossed paths at other car accidents. She threw her *angry-at-the-media-look* while I worked around the accident's permitted areas. I took pictures of the police officers and their investigation, and the firefighters and EMS workers digging through the car. Shattered glass surrounded them.

I felt like a parasite consuming the blood of good people. The helpers, like the EMS worker, made my soul crumble like the newspaper business. Confusion shuffling my thoughts, I did everything to emotionally detach from wrecks and other "*if it bleeds, it leads*" stories. While crying and drinking a third glass of the cheapest red wine the night after the accident, I nearly fell off my brown sofa laughing when I learned the house the car had hit belonged to a city council candidate in the middle of the campaign season. The candidate, meditating in his contemplation t-shirt and shorts, barely heard the crash. He was listening to mood music when the car rammed into the side of his home.

A few days later, the driver died. A month later, the candidate was elected. One week after that, a urine pregnancy test surprised me with a plus sign.

~ § ~

In the hot political season between September

and November, my nights as a news writer in North Carolina sometimes ran late. Every day proved unpredictable. But I craved such a career.

While I was employed for the five-day-a-week newspaper, I shut down all living operations except breathing and work involved with the job. A psychologist in high school told me: *It's not enough to survive. You have to live.* I thought choosing journalism meant I would be envied by others stuck behind their desks. I struggled to perfect the non-emotion reaction serious reporters learned: *You are not a part of the story. People need to know information from you. Get it together.* I aided the lesson with alcohol.

~ § ~

Now I had a new schedule to think about; the schedule of a journalist would not mesh with a child's day-to-day needs. I wondered if I had subconsciously sabotaged my hard news career.

On the commute to work each day, I cried. I cried at lunch. Back home, I sobbed before falling asleep, and woke up in tears. Stories like the meditating politician might make me smile a few minutes, but wine couldn't stop my weeping, just like it couldn't stop fires, robbery, abuse, or blood.

I had been diagnosed with depression in high school, yet I'd stayed off medication for two years. But with the first trimester of my pregnancy, my moods and emotions surged.

News of a child drove the dagger deeper into plans of a newsroom career. The publisher believed, I thought, in my ability to learn and adapt. I was a daughter of the late twentieth century; a modern woman. Then I thought of daycare. I wondered what place would keep my child those ten and eleven o'clock nights.

I was assigned stories about the county's ten percent unemployment rate. I saw full chairs and people standing against the walls inside unemployment offices as, one by one, factories closed or operated with minimum employees in Cleveland and Catawba Counties. I thought of my friends finding a tougher march to the job market than the path to graduation.

Meanwhile, I had a job with benefits I wanted to trash. I wanted to become something different; someone who could make a difference. If I couldn't be a serious journalist, maybe I should rekindle my hope to pursue a career as a middle school teacher.

But it wasn't only my news career that I mourned when the plus sign appeared on the pregnancy test stick. A chill froze my blood and whitened my already pale skin and I cried. I thought, *It'll be twenty years until I'm an author.* My Dad's sister once told me, "*Good writers experience life and aren't published until their forties.*" I didn't want to wait. I was not meant to have children now. Not when I had begun a writing career. In the process of writing for the newspaper, I stopped writing the novel I had worked on since my third year in college.

Within four months, I quit writing creative fiction, deserted cooking and talking to friends and family. Pregnancy hadn't stopped the creative flow. I did.

I debated abortion. But with a growing hand-to-wine-glass habit and disdain for my job, I knew it would send me off a cliff. In late November 2009, I gave my one-month notice and moved home to South Carolina.

My boyfriend, John, assured me I would complete the book. Time would exist for the pen and keyboard. I'd finish the novel that idealist reporter's dream of, the one I'd researched and worked on for so long. I knew it would take a few more years before I was ready to find a literary agent. I needed to finish the book.

~ § ~

For nine months, I worked as a substitute teacher, wrote and edited my novel. The baby's feet kicked ribs. It became harder to sit in a chair for more than twenty minutes. Fear stirred the heart. A real human would come out of me. I wondered if I would make a good mother. Selfish in my desire and need to compose, motherhood made me more curious than any investigation.

John and I took classes at the hospital. I practiced deep breaths and pictured myself somewhere else besides labor. A nurse, who had given birth to nine children, taught other us how to meditate. She also preached cloth diapers and saving the placenta. She told us she had kept all nine placentas from her childbirths, and she and her husband planted each of them with a tree. I was never one for gardens, but she taught me the meditation techniques I needed. Despite the fact I'd never been in labor, I figured pain would ram into me.

I wanted to be the meditating city council candidate on my son's big day. I recalled how calm he was when I interviewed him after the *car rammed his house.* Deep breath—the kind singers take before they hold a long note— went in and out of my lungs. I prepared for so long I thought the labor pains would never begin. John recorded minutes between contractions. They felt like a spike plunging into my ribs and then pulled out for two minutes. It went on for hours until we arrived at the hospital. I thought of happy things, a focal point, or how I wanted everyone in the room to hush as the pain grew. *Breathing, keep breathing*, I thought as the nurse measured labor pains by minutes. After two hours, or so it seemed, the nurses offered the happy medicine.

On June 15, 2010, I learned magic existed. Everyone else who denied its wonder was wrong. The crying, wet ball of red skin and cherry kissed yellow hair was my son. The actions in the delivery room happened so fast that I remember little, but I recalled his hair sticking up in every direction. As happy as I felt, I recognized his fear. He had lived in a warm nine-month haven. I'd felt him, but I had not seen or heard him. I refused to admit my own selfish fear that day.

The writing was done.

My grandmother later told me, *Things happen in life. You shouldn't feel that way over a book.* The click of fingers tapping the keyboard was a need. It had nothing to do with thirst, shelter, or hunger, but it was an absolute *need* for living and survival. I hated the writer's cliché: *I must write to live.* It would not be a cliché if it weren't true.

Thoughts raced through my head in the days following Charles' birth. Lack of sleep and a touch of postpartum depression made me wonder. Some boyfriends abandoned their girlfriends before or after she gave birth. A single mom was left to work more than one job, earn a degree or two, and raise a child. Little time was left for the child, let alone a mother's hobby or passion.

John left his former wife and faced his family's complete rejection. He made a new career for himself and us.

"I would not support you if your writing was simply a hobby or not any good," he said, "but I think you are truly a great writer."

The first month after Charles' birth passed as slow as the last ninety-minute class in high school. I was not eating the extra five hundred calories required to breastfeed him. Part of my teenage depression included an eating disorder, and it continued to haunt me. Lost energy and sleep also caused me lose my appetite. I did not realize what it would cost. After listening to several breastfeeding lectures, Charles and I made a good team. Seven times a day and twenty minutes on each breast exhausted me. It left little energy to sit in front of a laptop. I switched to a hard book and notepaper. I wrote with my left hand as much as my right while I breastfed him. I switched hands when he switched breasts. I also read to him from my favorite novels.

If I was not breastfeeding, I pumped breast milk. I felt like a machine. John worked, changed diapers, and did laundry. I fed and pumped and fed and pumped. The baby's appetite grew. At two months, my breasts did not produce the amount he needed. In my mind, I heard the breastfeeding Nazi voices: *A good mother breastfeeds. Formula will never be as good. Breastfed children are much smarter and healthier.* I did not believe all these things, yet I felt them.

My heart broke. Although I had begun feeling like a machine, Charles and I found a way to make writing and breastfeeding work. What hurt the most was not being able to feed my child the way I wanted. I did not understand the reasons why my milk stopped producing a regular amount, but he required more nourishment.

In the following months, Charles and I strolled on the Riverwalk next to the Catawba River. I parked his stroller. He napped and I wrote. I began writing beyond the contents of my novel. Short stories and truths evolved on the page whether it was crap or good material. I continued to scrawl a pen over blue lined pages. Words evolved, and I believed I had found a way. I could become a teacher. I could be a good mother, and I would remain a writer.

Wonder and Humility: One Mother in Florence—Ann V. Klotz

From the rooftop garden, I note sounds of morning traffic near the Arno, the whoosh of trucks on cobblestones through these impossibly narrow, ancient streets. Our suitcases, jammed full of leather gloves and marbled paper, bulge downstairs, awaiting our departure.

Florence is like a punctuation mark, delineating chapters in our family. First, when we longed for children; next, with two daughters, five and seven, together in every photo. Now, with Atticus, too, and his sisters. Miranda has been dancing in Florence, a demanding three-week program to supplement her dance major. Cordelia is in that hideous limbo between the end of high school and the start of college. Atticus turns nine in Florence, climbing to the top of the Duomo to celebrate, happy to eat pasta at every meal, but suspicious of the lovely *torta* produced by the baker in Greve—it is chocolate and filled with cream, but when he bites what we mistake for a frosting rose, he spits out a petal of hard red plastic. Suspicions confirmed, he pushes his plate away.

This time, the streets feel mysterious—coffered ceilings spied from the street through un-shuttered windows, peeling stucco, enormous wooden doors and facades that conceal lives inside. Florence becomes the metaphor for family—a series of contrasts and paradoxes. The smell of warm, fresh pizza overlaid by a faint scent of sewage. After dinner, the plazas are filled with vendors launching tiny, glowing whirligigs—neon plastic in the velvet sky: ancient and modern; enduring and tacky; what we think a family ought to be and what it is.

Without a working GPS and interpreting ambiguous directions, my husband, the intrepid driver, and Cordelia, triumphant navigator, discover the gates to our villa in Greve. We press a button and are admitted by Morena, our charming, non-English speaking caretaker. I am conscious of the luxury of being without responsibility, without language, even. We manage—gestures, repetition and good will. On the terrace of the villa, Tuscany unfurls around me. A perfect setting—cool stone floors, plaster walls, lots of chintz, photos of another family. It is our family that feels full of fissures. We spill our belongings into the lovely house, the detritus of laptop cords, phone chargers, maps, shoes, plastic animals, guidebooks, sunblock strewn everywhere. Chaos: our normal state, achieved immediately. Reunited with Miranda, we play house— shopping at an outdoor market, eating cheese and figs. I thought the setting would change us, but we have brought ourselves with us—each one a complicated, irregular piece of a jigsaw puzzle intended to be whole, but hard to fit together.

~ § ~

We are hot. It is, after all, Italy in July. On top of each other, literally, in our small rental car, we explore San Gimignano and Siena, hilly one-lane roads, complicated rotaries with indecipherable signage. I love the vineyards, the light, the landscape. I try to tune out the grumpiness emanating from the back seat.

Both girls text continuously; when reception fails on winding roads, I am gleeful and they are cross. I am grateful for their physical presence but jealous to have been supplanted in their affections for hours at a time. I judge them harshly, the way they judge me when my job trumps family. Guilty, I overcompensate, falsely cheerful. I annoy even myself.

We are prone to huge bursts of feeling—tears, sarcasm, laughter, scorn. Like summer thunderstorms without warning, moods shift. Tempers erupt then subside. Injuries abound: twisted ankles, scraped knees (mine, as I tumble off a curb), bug bites, an infected ear piercing that must be tended to immediately in the square in San Gimignano, gelato in one hand, hydrogen peroxide in the other. We are the wounded and the comforters, the source of anxiety and the balm. Is this what it is to be a family? Swings from miraculous to mundane, from delight to terror?

"What?" demands a daughter. "Why are you looking at me like that?"

Fighting back tears, (why is it that my daughters know precisely how to wound me?) I struggle to remember that I am the mom, the grown up, that they feel secure enough to show me their underbellies, that they don't intend their barbs to do such damage.

The fact is they wound my pride. I'm an expert in adolescent girls—everyone else's adolescent girls, that is. I'm the Head of a girls' school—for twenty-nine years I have specialized in girls—teaching them, listening, loving, standing for reality, using humor to help girls weather the inevitable trials of adolescence, reassuring anxious parents, learning to act unsurprised, calm, steady. I enjoy teenage girls. I get them. And many of them trust me, like me back. How can I be so confident, so certain of my instincts with other people's daughters and so faltering with my own?

Expertise helps very little when the girls across the table belong to me. Love is tangled with expectations, with my sense that I should know just what to say and do to diffuse their cross audacity. A wise colleague once suggested my threshold for shock was too high with my own kids; because I had seen so much, it took a lot to make me react. "Act more dismayed," he counseled. Now the distress feels authentic. In those parenting books stacked by my bed when the girls were small, I knew my toddlers were on track developmentally when they could grasp Cheerios with thumb and forefinger. Smug then, I laughed at much of the information in those tomes, preferring common sense and the wisdom of others who had gone before me.

Now, in Italy, I find myself longing for such a volume to descend, telling me precisely what to do in these tense moments. Retreat is insufficient. I take a deep breath.

"Don't give them so much power," I chide myself. I muse at pigeons nesting high up on the Duomo. "Let go," I incant, feeling only slightly insane as I float above my family, in the grip of another furious restaurant skirmish.

"Lower your expectations," I recall my older sister's mantra that difficult evening when we trample each other's hearts over gluten-free pasta. "Rules for parenting: Breathe. Feed them. Don't take everything so personally."

"It will not always feel like this," I coach myself. We love each other so, yet we are so hard on one another. No one can let anything go. Everyone has to be right. To reconcile my image of what this time ought to be with what it is feels hard. Where is the golden glow I expected Italy to rain down on all of us?

I focus on the good, the wonder: the half hour in Venice when we surrender to the gondola, glad of the breeze and the gondolier's banter, unashamed tourists; the cool sweetness of cinnamon gelato; Atticus crumpled, damp, asleep in the back of the car, leaning against willing sisters; bells pealing everywhere on the quarter hour.

I wonder if the bells, like sirens, become the background. Must wonder melt to matter of fact? My own thrill at holding newborn infants morphed as they grew into beings with opinions and moods. There is wonder, still, of course. I marvel at how my daughters are each other's harshest critics and most loyal advocates. My breath catches when Cordelia calls us all back from a quarrel, reminding us that it frightens Atticus when we fight. When, after I have scraped my knee, my daughters urge me into an expensive shop because in the window they have seen the kind of leather boxes I keep my earrings in. I remember these moments when the girls snarl and snap like feral cats. We love each other. We do the best we can.

The formality of the Boboli Gardens disappoints Atticus, who wanted a park with flowers and a playground. Using the map, we cajole him, locating lemon trees on an island in the middle of a pond, feathers scummy on murky water. It is disgusting, but strangely lovely. The mazes are not really mazes, just fancy paths of tall boxwood. Atticus hurtles down an allée—a long leafy arch. As they did in childhood, Cordelia and Miranda claim to be princesses. It is easy to imagine the sweep of silk along these paths; I wonder if the Medici girls, down through the centuries, were given to fits of pique that annoyed their mothers.

Our last night, we wander to the piazza in front of San Spirito's austere façade and eat at Miranda's favorite trattoria. Afterwards, Atticus joins a game of pick-up soccer in the square. We watch him playing with several Italian children, two toddlers who get in everybody's way, and an American boy, who organized the game and welcomed Atticus to the fray. This is the moment for me to remember—parents and sisters smiling at this sweaty boy engaged in a glorious, spontaneous, joyful game.

Atticus appears on the rooftop—in pajamas,

his features blurry, proud of having discovered me. Wonder: early morning in Florence, embracing a newly nine-year-old son, looking out at the campanile next door, the day full of possibility—no blame, no sorrow.

Within the hour, the anxiety of travel brings out the worst in each of us. There are penalties for extra bags. I fuss, overly apologetic; Miranda and Cordelia, in a tussle over who holds the boarding passes, prompt my usually mild husband to anger; he is the steady force around which we all typically arrange ourselves, but his grim face shuts us out. His mood is glacial. He insists we must spend every Euro on pizza no one has the appetite to eat. Atticus grips my hand. Eventually, we are tucked into our seats, sardine-style, homeward bound. I do needlepoint, soothed by the undemanding basket weave. A few hours into the journey, apologies are uttered; anger melts into Lufthansa upholstery. Sometimes a trans-Atlantic flight can heal even a fractious family. Sometimes a mother can beat up on herself a little bit less and love her family just as they are.

The Day That Changed My Life Forever—Rita Reynolds Setness

December 20th, 2013 started just like any other day. I got up early that morning because I had a lot of things to prepare for our holiday get-together with my family. I took the time to make my usual breakfast and sit down with the paper. Nothing untoward, or in any way unusual about the day, no warning of the abrupt shift our lives would take in less than an hour.

I made my breakfast and sat down in my chair with the paper. My son Jonathon came up from the basement where his room was and got a trash bag and some cleaning supplies. He stood in the doorway of the kitchen and talked to me for a few minutes. I asked him if he was still going to make a cheese ball for our get-together. He was an awesome cook and loved to make yummies for people to enjoy. He agreed that he was and I asked him what he was doing. He said he was going to clean his room and I raised an eyebrow and asked him, "What was the occasion?" He shrugged his shoulders, smiled and said, "Just random." We chatted another minute or so and he started to go downstairs.

He paused and looked back at me and I could only see his head as he was down a couple of stairs and said he had changed his mind and was going to the holiday get-together after all. A couple of days before he had decided not to go, so I was happy that he was going. Then he went on downstairs and I went to get a cup of coffee and finished reading the paper. When I was done, I went to tell Jonathon that I was going to take a shower and go get my nails done. I went to the head of the stairs and called his name. No answer, I called again and still nothing. I sighed and, figuring that he was back in his room and could not hear me, went down to find him.

In his room, I saw evidence of cleaning but no Jonathon. I went to open the door that led from the family room into the laundry room but when I went to push it open, something was holding it closed. I looked down and saw Jonathon's head was on the floor wedged between the door and the freezer behind it.

I yelled his name and got no response. Things start to get hazy and foggy here and I think God uses that fog to protect us from losing our minds. I remember trying to get in to him and I remember climbing over him onto the freezer. I got down off the freezer and shook him but he was totally limp and his eyes were half-open. I screamed his name and tried to check and see if he was breathing. I did not have my phone and though I hated with everything in me to leave him I knew I had to call for help so I climbed back over him and ran upstairs.

I burst into my bedroom and screamed for my husband who was still asleep, since he works nights. He jumped up and ran downstairs with me right on his heels. He managed to move Jonathon a little bit and get in the room with him but I could not get in and did not want to disturb the CPR he was attempting. I was on the phone with 911 trying to relay what they were saying to my husband and telling them what information I was getting from him.

I could barely choke out words, as there was absolutely no moisture in my mouth or throat. I have no idea what I said or what they said, I was probably hysterical. I know I was screaming a lot. The dispatcher told me to go meet the EMTs so I ran back upstairs to the front porch, praying with every ounce of will I had. My neighbor pulled up and, seeing my face, asked me what was wrong. I told her Jonathon was not breathing, she asked where he was and took off running as I led her to him. Then I ran back up to wait for the paramedics. When they got there, I led them down to Jonathon and my neighbor came out reassuring me that she had found a pulse. I sank into her with relief, crying.

A female paramedic came out of the laundry

room and I asked her if he was breathing. She looked at me like I was crazy and said, "No," very sharply and very abruptly. I started screaming. I was losing my mind. I had to be losing my mind. This had to be some kind of crazy nightmare.

The ambulance got Jonathon to the hospital and I ran in the front door to the reception area. I don't remember much, just screaming, "Is he alive? Is he alive?" over and over again. The receptionist had no information, but eventually we were led back to a room wait. There was an altar with a Bible, and I knelt to feverishly pray the same thing over and over, "Please God! Don't take him! Take me, not him!" My parents arrived and sat with us. Eventually, the Doctor came in and said some gibberish that made absolutely no sense to me. I looked in his face, trying desperately to make sense of what he was saying to me, but I could not make it out, so I asked him if Jonathon was going to be OK. He looked at me harshly and said, "Do you not understand what I am saying to you?"

I was just sitting on the floor, looking at him and could not take it in. He tried to tell me that Jonathon was not going to make it, and was already gone.

I later learned that every time they stopped working Jonathon's heart for him, it stopped beating. But at the time, what he was saying made no sense to me. None of it made sense to me. I was JUST talking to him and he was fine! How? Why?

They took me back to him, and I can still see him lying there, feet limp and sticking out sideways, motionless as they worked on him. The Doctor said some more gibberish and I still could not tell you what he said, but I knew that Jonathon, my precious, beautiful, smart, loving, giving Jonathon was gone. I told them to stop what they were doing and they did. I think the only reason they were still doing it was for my benefit, not his, and I could not stand to see them doing all this stuff to him for no reason.

I was in shock. I was totally in shock. I could not take in what had happened. I walked around in a fog for days. The funeral planning, the visitation, the funeral...all a fog. I look back and cannot comprehend a lot of what went on. I know I was there. I remember standing by Jonathon's coffin, looking at his beautiful face, stroking his cheek over and over. I could not bear to leave his side for a second. I could not eat. I could barely drink. It is so hard to swallow when you are so filled with pain you feel you are going to throw up.

I survived those first few days by the grace of God. God gave me things to focus on, at the most unlikely of times. At the hospital, my other two sons came to me, broken and sad, needing me and my comfort. As a mother, you manage to put some of your sorrow aside to comfort your children and I was able to do that. I held them and comforted them in their pain, and God gave me the strength to do that through the funeral process. When they were overcome, I was able to be there for them.

At the funeral, I was just a walking, breathing, shell. They asked me if I wanted to help shut the coffin and I did want to do this last thing for my son. After closing the coffin, I almost fell, stumbling back to my seat, but God gave me the strength to make it. Sitting in the pew between my two sons, I tried to listen to the service. It is mostly a blur to me, but I remember laying my head over on my youngest son's shoulder and, looking up at the wall behind where the choir sits, there was a blue banner, with one word, all in silver, sparkly caps: HOPE. I stared, fixated. HOPE. HOPE. HOPE.

It was a beginning for me as I sat there at the end of our normal family life. HOPE. Jeremiah 29:11 says, "For I know the plans I have for you, declares the Lord, Plans to prosper you and not to harm you, plans to give you HOPE and a future." Along with the word HOPE, this verse continually popped out at me. Everywhere I went, everywhere I looked, this verse was there and became the theme of my grief process:

Trust in God and His plan for our lives.

HOPE for the future.

HOPE in knowing that Jonathon is alive in Heaven and I will see him again.

HOPE, always.

Wrestling with Myself—Julia Poole

On a winter evening, I sat in my parked 4 Runner, alone. From the radio, top 40 tunes droned. Blowing snow swirled around bundled parents walking from the parking lot toward the high school building. No sense waiting any longer. After dreading this night for days, I rallied the courage to move. Slamming the 4 Runner door, I crunched across the snow-covered parking lot and then hustled through the door. A short line of parents stood ahead. I waited behind them, brushing snow from my hair. Soon I was next.

"Welcome to West Catholic," said an older woman sitting behind a table. Without answering, I handed her five dollars, the entry fee for the wrestling meet.

Truth be told, I felt a bit cheated. Parents of other teen athletes watch their kids play elegant sports like tennis where kids barely break a sweat lobbing a ball across a net. Even the hard-knocking aggressiveness of football seemed tame compared to the hand-to-hand combat of wrestling. Intellectually, I understood wrestling was an old, noble sport—the ancient Greeks wrestled—but this knowledge had no influence on my current view that wrestling was just a step above boxing in the sporting world, a brutal blue-collar sport for thugs.

I moved toward the open gym doorway. Poor fluorescent lighting cast an unnatural glow. Pungent sweat, a permanent odor no disinfectant can remove, hung in the air. Fans filled bleachers on both sides of the gym. Loud chatter competed with unintelligible rap songs that cranked through the scratchy sound system. A large mat taped to the gym floor served as a reminder of the battles to take place. I cursed aloud, angry with my husband, Jeff, for traveling on business instead of standing here at my side.

~ § ~

Six weeks earlier, as our family sat together for a weeknight meal—a rare occurrence in our busy lives— Alex made an announcement.

"I signed up for the wrestling team today."

Avoiding eye contact, Alex's hands grabbed a bowl of mashed potatoes. The sound of plopping spuds filled an empty silence. A second helping I knew he would never eat. Alex never ate second helpings of anything.

"What did you say?" I asked. *Why would you do that?*

Caroline, Alex's little sister giggled. Fourteen-year-old Alex had never wrestled a day in his life.

"I joined the wrestling team."

"Why wrestling?" Jeff asked. I envied his self-control.

"Wrestling or bowling. It was simple. They cut people on the bowling team, but not in wrestling. I'm *guaranteed* to wrestle."

Alex twirled his fork in the middle of the mashed potatoes as if they were spaghetti noodles, boring a hole the size of a quarter in the center of the spuds. Not another morsel of food entered Alex's mouth or mine even as whiffs of baked chicken drifted above the kitchen table. When nervous, Alex and I lost our appetites. We were alike in this way. At the time, I couldn't discern the exact cause of Alex's apprehension. I assumed he was nervous about telling us his wrestling plans or perhaps felt anxious about trying the sport. I had never given much thought to wrestling before, but now I felt an intense dislike of the sport, a feeling I did not immediately understand.

Alex flourished while in middle school, participating in organized sports, school plays, and student council. Acclimating to high school, where he knew no one, proved difficult. Alex studied and spent time with the family, but he chose not to participate in school activities outside the classroom, his social life nonexistent. Now, Alex's life seemed out of sync, always a step behind, one sentence too late to a conversation. Worried, we encouraged Alex to join a club or winter sport, hoping involvement would spark a bit of happiness.

Alex took our advice to heart.

"Do you know what you have to do when you wrestle? It's one-on-one…in front of everyone," said Jeff.

"Yeah, I know. Coach says he can teach me everything I need to know. He seemed pretty excited that I joined the team."

I looked at my son's lanky frame; barely five feet tall and 93 pounds. If Coach saw wrestling potential, I failed to share his opinion.

"Practice starts Wednesday."

Jeff congratulated Alex and continued speaking about wrestling using words like "discipline" and "character builder". Feeling nauseated by the thought of Alex wrestling, I stood at the counter, scraping cold potatoes from Alex's plate into the trash.

~ § ~

Unaware that wrestling parents stick together, I overlooked the cluster of Catholic Central faithful planted in a small section of bleachers. A sea of royal blue, this oasis beckoned amidst the landscape of West Catholic green jackets and sweatshirts. I was too nervous to notice and remained rooted in the gym doorway.

On and around the mat, groups of boys stretched or jogged in place. Paired boys wrangled together in helter-skelter fashion across the mat. Laughing and joking, the boys seemed at ease. Some sported five o'clock shadows and weighed two hundred to almost three hundred pounds. A few sprouted hair from their backs and chests. Was all that body hair legal in a sport like wrestling?

I spied Alex sitting on the edge of the mat performing a series of stretches. He appeared calm, composed. Even so, my heart raced faster, anxiety building. I took deep breaths.

A shrill whistle blew. Alex and his teammates took seats in folding chairs surrounding an outer edge of the mat. The boys in green jogged out of the gym. Confused, I thought perhaps they were leaving school. The gym lights dimmed. Conversation ceased. A whooshing sound blasted over the sound system before a funky DA-DA-DA…DA-DA-DA-DA-DA…DA-DA-DA beat punctuated the silence. One by one, members of the host team—the guys in green—made their triumphant entry back into the gym, hoods pulled up, and arms waving to their cheering fans in the stands. It was impossible to hear the announcer above whistles and shouts from the crowd or the deafening rally call of DA-DA-DA…Y'ALL READY FOR THIS? High school wrestling felt more like game three of the NBA finals.

~ § ~

A real coup by Coach, Alex was the lone boy to wrestle in the 103-pound weight class. The fact that Alex weighed ten pounds less bothered me, but not Coach. No time wasted wrestling junior varsity, freshman Alex vaulted to varsity status. I did not share Coach's enthusiasm.

Thinking Alex would change his mind about this whole wrestling thing once he went to a few practices, I tried not to worry much. Practice lasted two hours every day after classes at the athletic facility located some eight miles from school.

"I can pick you up from school and drive you to practice," I said.

Driving Alex home after practice, I noticed his face glistened with sweat. A fleeting image of Alex thrashing on filthy mats teaming with germs almost made me gag.

"Mom, I'm going with the guys."

"What guys?"

"You know, the juniors and seniors on the team. The guys who *drive*."

"Are they good drivers?" I paused, "You should offer these boys money for taking you, don't you think?"

"That's not how it's done. These guys are going to practice anyway. They don't want money. They said when I'm older, I'll do the same for the younger guys." Sighing, looking out the passenger window, Alex turned to me and asked, "Heard a great joke today, want to hear it?"

As I listened to the joke, I wanted to ask, *What about the pain factor? What about the possibility of getting hurt? What about the even stronger possibility of failing in front of a gym full of people?* I never asked these questions, because I knew Alex was contemplating them on his own. Much like me, Alex spent considerable time analyzing the what-ifs of life.

~ § ~

Each team assembled in a circle, heads bowed together, arms around each other's shoulders. Chants of "Go Green!" and "Go CC!" echoed. From each team, a unison clap of hands signaled solidarity. The thumping music cut abruptly. Everyone stood for the playing of the National Anthem. Spotting an open seat on a bottom bleacher, I stepped into place, applauding with everyone upon hearing "…and the home of the brave!"

The announcer stated matches would begin at the 119-pound weight class. A boy from each team stripped their warm-ups and, after grabbing headgear and mouthpieces, approached the scoring table. Before this moment, I had not seen a wrestler in uniform up close. Soccer, rugby, baseball, basketball, hockey, and football—the uniforms of these sports had a certain rugged, honorable quality to them. Nothing about the wrestling singlet screamed majestic or handsome. Like a leotard with shorts, the skintight Lycra fabric of a singlet hugged every muscle and crevice. Functional, yes, but the boys looked like oversized ballerinas without tutus, a complete fashion disaster.

The two boys approached the center of the mat where the ref stood waiting. Crouching in a neutral position, the wrestlers faced each other with outstretched arms, anticipating the sound of the whistle. Unable to remain still, one boy inched forward and back, his pent-up energy barely contained, like a snake recoiling and trembling before striking its prey.

I wanted to turn away, but a stronger urge took over. No different from anyone else, I wanted to see what would happen next. The ref blew the whistle.

Then the real chaos began.

Several people rose around me, blocking my view. Deafening screams filled the gym. I wanted to say, *quiet down and sit so I can pay attention!* Frustrated, I found myself standing on tiptoe, stretching forward to snatch a look at the battle on the mat.

The wrestlers began circling each other, looking to attack, dancing to an unheard rhythm, heads bobbing and arms jabbing. The boy in green grabbed the other's forearms and moved his feet forward in an effort to trip him. The strategy worked. In the next instant, the boy in royal blue fell, smacking to the mat with the other boy atop of him. A classic takedown, I would later learn. Wrangling mano-a-mano, the boy in royal blue scrambled, his feet and hands clawing in a vain effort to get out from under the green boy's clutches. At the same time, green boy exerted all the force he could muster to maintain his superior position. A mass of strained muscles, purple and red-hued faces, slaps of skin, squeaks of rubber shoes and guttural groans combined to form a clash of cacophonic proportions. Never had I been so close to humans fighting with such physical intensity.

Feeling disgusted, I listened as fans shouted words of encouragement from all corners of the gym.

"Drive…*DRIVE…DRIIIIVE!*"

"Be…*TOUGH…*"

"Get-*EM…GET HIM…*"

Struggling, the royal blue boy could not escape. The green boy now had the royal blue boy on his back with one leg bent in a tight clutch. Holding an outstretched arm, applying every inch of force and weight at his disposal, green boy pressed upon the chest of the fallen boy, squeezing his shoulder blades into the mat. A pin in the making, this seemed more like an act of torture than a clean wrestling move, but the ref did nothing to stop the match. Spine arched high, flopping back and forth, the boy struggled to escape the inevitable loss, much as a gasping fish looks as it bounces on a dock trying to splash its way back into water. Lying on the mat, the ref inspected the shoulder blades of the floundering boy. In one final stroke, the ref slapped his hand on the mat. Whistle blown, match over. The green boy scored six points, a perfect pin.

Standing, green boy extended a hand to his vanquished foe, a sign of reconciliation. Still on his back, the royal blue boy reached up, clasping the offered hand. Once standing, breaths heaving, the boys shook hands. Small bursts of applause began to trickle through the crowd. As the ref raised the hand of the green boy, roars of praise for the wrestler's performance erupted from the bleachers.

Alex stood with his other teammates, clapping in a show of support as the defeated wrestler took his seat two chairs from Alex. The 125-

pound wrestlers sprinted to the scoring table. I performed the mental math. Alex would wrestle second to last.

Within seconds, the next match began. Time groaned forward. Each match started and finished in much the same way as the first. A blur of flexing muscles, strained limbs and unnatural, pained facial expressions came and went. Wrestlers' eyes chronicled the conflicts. Those eyes. Some appeared wild with aggressiveness, a willingness to win at all cost. Other eyes registered a bit of fear, a cry of surrender, the blink of inescapable loss. I wondered what other parents saw in their sons' eyes when they wrestled. What destiny would Alex's eyes convey?

Soon Alex stood behind his teammates, hopping side-to-side, swinging his arms back and forth. Warming up, Alex looked no different from other boys. But other boys were not my son. Watching Alex at this moment, I heard his infant cry. I tasted his first ice cream cone as it dribbled down his smiling face. I smelled the waters of Lake Michigan in his hair as I wrapped his wet, shivering body in a beach towel. I felt the zip of Alex's life force through the grasp of his tiny hand holding mine while crossing streets.

~ § ~

On his way home from work, Jeff often picked up Alex after wrestling practice. Sometimes arriving early, he would venture inside to check out the practices. Coach said Alex was a hard worker, a fast learner. Coach assured Jeff that he would not put Alex in unnecessary matches if the opponent looked highly skilled. I thought, compared to Alex, everyone must have more experience and certainly more skill. Many boys wrestled for years before entering high school.

I feared for Alex's safety.

Whenever I questioned the safety of the sport, Jeff said, "Alex is learning the basic wrestling moves. He seems to like it. Don't worry so much…Alex will be fine."

Jeff's reassuring words did not stop worst-case scenarios from haunting my overactive imagination. Visions whirled of grunting, sumo-sized wrestlers laughing with glee while thrusting skinny Alex high in the air before slamming him with ruthless malice. Ambulance sirens added great dramatic effect. How could Alex compete with experienced wrestlers ten pounds heavier? I attempted to beef up Alex's caloric intake, hoping to add a couple of pounds to his slight frame, but Alex expended so much energy training that he did not gain an ounce. I had no control over the situation at all.

~ § ~

Peeling off his warm-ups and throwing them in a pile, Alex strode over to the scorer's table like a seasoned pro. Coach and a few other boys in royal blue clapped and shouted words like, "Alex, man…you can do it!" and "Go get-em, Alex!"

A boy emerged from the sidelines, high-fiving each green teammate before sprinting to the scorer's table. A number of people in the bleachers rose and started clapping. Alex shared the same height as his opponent, but the similarities ended there. Like a mini-Schwarzenegger, man-boy's muscles rippled over his body. He zipped to the center of the mat—waist bent, torso hunched forward—but unlike other wrestlers, this guy slapped his hands upside his headgear like some battle cry to his adoring fans. The chanting crowd grew louder with shouts of "Get-'em!" and "Pin, pin, pin, pin, pin!" Alex faced his opponent without blinking.

No longer could I hide from the truth. I wanted to stop the match by walking out there, grabbing Alex, and whisking him away. Although I worried about Alex's safety, I feared something more. The truth was, if Alex lost, I would feel shame, embarrassment and failure. In that moment, I realized the concern I directed toward Alex masked my anxiety, my fear that his failure would somehow be my failure. I wrestled with the idea in my mind, but felt incapable of untangling the mess. Paralyzed, I sat without uttering a word, my hands suddenly chafed and hot by the constant friction of wringing them over and over again.

The ref blew the whistle. Man-boy stealthily moved in circles, back hunched, his hands sharply jutting forward, slapping Alex's hands as if to say, "Hey, buddy, I'm about ready to make my move." Alex awkwardly followed man-boy, twice stubbing his left shoe on the mat, almost falling. Jerking his pointed hands forward, Alex strived to strike man-boy's hands, but each attempt failed. Eyes wide, Alex's slender frame nervously bounced as he tried to keep pace with man-boy. Alex's face screamed, "How the hell did I get into this?" It was the same scared-to-death look captured by the magic of flash photography at Cedar Point when Alex rode the Magnum roller coaster. After spending an hour in line, anticipating the fun ride ahead, Alex discovered the experience was more terrifying than entertaining. New experiences don't always turn out as expected.

Around me, the deafening noise magnified. Hearing Alex's name screamed from across the gym, I searched for the source. I discovered the cadre of Catholic Central parents jumping up and down, cheering on my son. I felt like an idiot, powerless.

Tiring of the cat and mouse game, with blazing speed and precision, man-boy grabbed Alex with two hands, hurled him on the mat—wham—and then lunged on top of him. With expert deftness, man-boy rolled Alex to his back, thrusting down on his chest using every ounce of body strength available. Like a pill bug on its back, Alex's limbs flailed in a useless effort to escape. The ref slid to mat-level, whistle poised in his mouth, and inspected man-boy's work before slapping his hand on the mat. The whistle shrieked. Releasing one long exhale of pent-up air, I felt immediate relief.

The pin took all of six seconds, a new school record for the green team. For me, the match seemed to drag on for minutes. The press reported the results. It was the first time Alex's name appeared in print.

Applause and hoots from the bleachers reverberated through the gym. Man-boy stood, offered a hand to Alex who still lay motionless on the mat. Accepting the gesture, Alex rose with resignation, sporting a look of defeat. Once standing, Alex shook hands with man-boy, returning to his seat as the ref raised man-boy's arm in victory.

Alex's team lost the meet by twenty-five points.

Slinking out of the gym, I hurried out the nearest exit, my heart still thumping at a too fast pace, my face flushed. Did I feel badly for what Alex had just gone through? Yes, but more than that, I felt heartbreaking guilt. Walking through the parking lot, this feeling swallowed me like a hungry dog that consumes a piece of meat without chewing it first and then, still hungry, looks for its next lump of food. My hunger for a clean conscience could not be satiated. Not coming through for my son, I was the ultimate loser, not Alex.

Sitting in the cold 4-Runner, I turned up the tunes and hummed along to Gnarls Barkley singing *Crazy*—"I remember when, I remember when I lost my mind…" Catching a glimpse of myself in the rearview mirror, a tired, middle-aged woman stared back, a mom, who, despite her flaws, loved her son.

The snow stopped falling. Boys emerged from the gym, some walking in small groups, some walking alone, some walking with parents. The heater started blowing warm air when Alex's shadowed figure left school. Head held high, Alex walked slowly, his backpack and athletic bag hanging low from his left shoulder.

"Hi, Alex. Rough match."

Alex threw his stuff behind and climbed in the passenger seat.

"Yeah, it's what I expected would happen."

"I'm sorry." *I can't express how sorry I feel.*

Pulling out of the snow-covered parking lot, I drove slowly toward the highway. A thin cover of glistening snow sparkled over parked cars, mailboxes and tree limbs.

"You don't have to do this. You don't have to wrestle."

I gave Alex an out, a predictable and

sympathetic parental gesture. I thought of how Alex never ate seconds. The selfish part of me hoped he would decide enough was enough, that trying this wrestling thing a second, third or fourth time was not worth the effort. But the self-sacrificing part of me knew how Alex would respond. I had always known.

"What do you mean? I can't quit now. I'm on the team. I get to wrestle *varsity.*"

"You got your butt kicked out there. That was hard to watch."

"I'll get better. I know I will. I'm not going to quit. I'm going to practice every day and someday…I'm going to win."

I said nothing and kept driving. My shortcomings had nothing to do with Alex. He didn't feel like a failure. For Alex, tonight's loss was a minor obstacle, the beginning of his high school wrestling experience. Alex would continue to test his limits in future endeavors, something he would do the rest of his life.

Yearning to peer into Alex's eyes, I wished to

express how humbled and inspired I felt by his positive spirit, perseverance and strength of character. A surge of determination flickered within. I could never relive the last two hours or become a rabid fan of wrestling, but I knew the day would come when a ref would raise Alex's arm in victory. Until that time, no matter how many losses Alex endured, I would be in the bleachers cheering his efforts. Perhaps then, I would be the winner Alex already was in my eyes.

To My Unborn Daughter and Her Brother Who's Already Creating Chaos on Earth—Amanda Etcheto

To the tiny avocado-sized human growing in my abdomen,

Someday you won't be blessed with innocent ignorance. You will cast aside belief in things like Santa Claus, Tinkerbell, and Mother Goose. The world you see beyond our front door will look nothing like the rosy picture your storybooks and Disney movies paint for you. Your brother wants to teach you how to train your own dragon, and I don't have it in me to tell him dragons don't exist. I'll let you believe that fairies sneak in and leave treasures for your teeth, and shooting stars are for wishing. I want you to believe in impossible things for as long as possible, to give you memories of happier times when the reality of the world becomes too much for your young shoulders.

When those days come, the darkness of the world will blot out the light in your wonder-filled eyes. When the chaos of day-to-day life mixes with heartbreaking agony from news stories and you question where the love has gone, I want you to remember the summer days of your youth. Remember the homemade ice pops and water fights, and your life as a mermaid, sword fighting away from the clutches of bumbling pirates. Remember your father's deep booming laughter, your mother's quiet smile, and your brother's annoying habit of knowing what to say to drive you crazy while letting you know he loves you. Never forget that Grandpa had more Star Wars toys than you, and Grandma made the best meatballs. Recollect the smell of cookies and eggnog on Christmas and the bellyaches from an overdose of Halloween candy. Remember the way it made you feel when your big brother taught you how to train your first night fury before you learned that real life was scarier than a dragon ever could be.

The happy memories get us through the hardest parts of life.

The world will steal the light in your eyes, but I'll be stealing bits of it back for safekeeping. A corner from a baby blanket, the tattered ear from a favored stuffed animal, first teeth, handprints, and too many photographs, memories safely tucked away in a few boxes for when you need them.

We probably won't be able to get you a brand new car when you get your license, or designer shoes, but our gifts will last longer, and be more useful. We want to give you a place to escape, a childhood filled with love, laughter and innocent ignorance, memories you can summon to remind you the love you thought was missing was with you all along. It's the best gift my parents gave to me, and if I've done my job it's one I will pass down to you.

For as long as we are here you can rely on

your logical, over-protective father to share his wealth of knowledge while defending your heart and honor with every bit the warrior's spirit of his D&D characters. You can cuddle with your hippie, overly affectionate mother when you need to, or when you just want cookies. And when we're not around anymore…well…that's a talk for a different day in a galaxy I hope is far, far away.

Love always,

The human incubator you will someday call Mommy.

Author Bios

Rebecca T. Dickinson works at a school in Charlotte, NC with students who are diagnosed with neurological disorders, and as a graduate assistant at Winthrop University. She researches and writes about educational technology. Dickinson has also worked as a reporter and freelance writer. Her freelance work has appeared in *Biz Well* publications, on *Tryon Plaza's* blog, and on the Law Related Education division of the South Carolina Bar's website. In October 2013 she received an Honorable Mention for her story *Left to Rust* in the Porter Fleming Literary Competition. Her writings have appeared in *The Copperfield Review, Black Fox Literary Magazine, Blue Ridge Literary Prose, Dew on the Kudzu,* and the anthologies *Impact,* and *PaniK: Candid Stories of Life Altering Experiences Surrounding Pregnancy.*

Amanda Etcheto is a mother of two, although some days she is certain her husband makes three, trying to balance the chaos of working in healthcare, going to college and maintaining a happy home for her budding family. While she may be losing the battle to keep her sanity, she's grounded by her belief in the impossible. As she tells her kids, she likes to keep a little bit of shimmery fairy dust tucked away for emergencies.

Oren Hammerquist's first novel, *Murphy's Second Death*, is available from most ebook sellers and select print retailers. He has been published in *Romance Magazine, Soldier Story anthology*, and several poetry journals. His next book is a collection of love stories with science fiction undertones titled *Love Transcends*. (Now available for preorder.) Originally from Seattle, Oren has spent the last eight years in the military in various countries and states—often away from his wife and three little girls. He is currently completing his MA in English and Creative writing at Southern New Hampshire University: College of Online and Continuing Education. In addition to writing, military service, and college studies, he is a self-appointed activist for online student pride and recognition. Find out more at www.orenhammerquist.com.

Treg Isaacson is a counselor in a university mental health clinic in Seattle. He has had other work published in *About Place Journal* and in the *Monarch Review*, where the paragraph entitled 'Sneaking' was originally seen. He was a featured reader in June 2014 at Old Growth Northwest. His connections to Kentucky are many, having grown up in Southern Illinois, where Kentucky is no more than a stone's throw across the Ohio. One of his best friends, a bandmate, grew up in Louisville, and they are certainly drawn to each other because of their origins and land of their hearts. Although he is a father, he feels the Motherlode. Follow Treg on Twitter @TregTregi.

Ann V. Klotz is the Head of Laurel School, an independent girls' school in Shaker Heights, OH. She writes most often about being a mother, a teacher, and a school leader. Her family—one patient husband, one young son, two college-age daughters, three rescue dogs and two cats—inspire her daily. Her work has appeared in *The Legendary*, *Community Works Institute Journal*, *Independent School*, and the *Huffington Post*, for which she blogs. Readers can email her at avk1223@yahoo.com or follow her on Twitter @AnnKlotz.

Andrea Lani is a writer, mother, human ecologist, and public servant. Her writing has appeared in *Orion, Kindred, Brain, Child Magazine, Literary Mama, About Place Journal*, and *Mutha Magazine*, and is forthcoming in *Snowy Egret* and *Northern Woodlands*. She lives in Maine with her husband and three sons. Find her online at www.remainsofday.blogspot.com.

Julia Poole has always carried a passion for writing, but it wasn't until she stepped away from a twenty-year career as a speech-language therapist that she began to pursue this passion with vigor. Julia was born and raised in Western Michigan, where she currently resides. She has a B.A. in Audiology & Speech Sciences and an M.A. in Speech-Language Pathology, both from Michigan State University. She is a member of the Oral History Association and the Association of Writers & Writing Programs, and writes memoir and creative nonfiction. Julia has two college-aged children and has been married for thirty years. "Wrestling with Myself" was previously published in *MOON Magazine* in May, 2014. Reach Julia at poole.11@outlook.com.

Michael Schofield is the father of children with schizophrenia. The Jani Foundation was founded by Michael and Susan Schofield. The foundation was named for their daughter, Jani, who was diagnosed with child onset schizophrenia at 6 years old. Michael and Susan felt alone in their struggle to keep Jani alive.

The Foundation's goal is "socialization over isolation," providing free social events for public school children classified "emotionally disturbed" (ED) and their families. It is a very simple idea: if you encourage social opportunities for ED/mentally ill children, you decrease the isolation on which the mental illness feeds on. We are teaching these kids that our community cares about them and that they are part of us. For more information, go to http://janifoundation.org. Buy Michael Schofield's book *January First: A Child's Descent into Madness and Her Father's Struggle to Save Her*, at online book retailers. Reach Michael at mschofield@janifoundation.org.

Tamara Kaye Sellman lives and writes in Bainbridge Island, WA. Find her on the web at www.tamarasellman.com.

Rita Reynolds Setness lost her son Jonathon in Dec. 2013 to natural causes, and will never, ever be the same. Her heart will always be broken, but God gives her strength to make it through each day. Rita works at Jessamine County Schools as a substitute teacher. She attended Eastern Kentucky University and lives in Nicholasville, KY. Read her small (hopefully) inspirational status every day at *Surviving Child Loss*, located at mothergrief.blogspot.com.

Stephanie Vanderslice is Professor of Writing at the University of Central Arkansas. She writes fiction and creative nonfiction and has published prose in many journals and anthologies, including *The American Literary Review, Writing-On-the-Edge, So-to-Speak* and *Knowing Pains: Women on Work, Sex and Love in their 40s* (featured on the Today show). She has also published three books on the teaching of creative writing, most recently *Rethinking Creative Writing*. Her column "The Geek's Guide to the Writing Life" appears regularly in the *Huffington Post*. Her fiction is represented by Anne Bohner of *Pen and Ink Literary*. Vanderslice lives north of Little Rock, Arkansas with her husband, writer John Vanderslice and their two sons. She can also bake a mean loaf of French bread, if you really want to know. Stephanie can be reached at stephv@uca.edu.

About the Editor

Ashley Parker Owens lives in the hills of Kentucky, where the gnomes are. She has lived in San Francisco in an ashram, and in Chicago where she helped with the Second Underground Press Conference and was the creator and editor of Global Mail. After the successful publication of *Gnome Harvest* by Double Dragon Publishing, Ashley is writing the next novels in the Gnome Stories Series, while obtaining an MFA in Creative Writing at Eastern Kentucky University. She also has an MFA from Rutgers University in Visual Arts.

To submit works for a future anthology, go to
http://kystory.net.

16264638R00103

Made in the USA
San Bernardino, CA
25 October 2014